Voices of Victorian London

Voices of Victorian London

In Sickness and In Health

Henry Mayhew

Published by Hesperus Press Limited
19 Bulstrode Street, London W1U 2JN
www.hesperuspress.com

London Labour and the London Poor first published in 1851
This edition first published by Hesperus Press Limited, 2011
Foreword © Jonathan Miller, 2011

Designed and typeset by Fraser Muggeridge studio
Printed in Jordan by Jordan National Press

ISBN: 978-1-84391-350-4

Contents

Foreword

In the inquiring mind of Henry Mayhew we are beginning to see the antecedents of social anthropology, the process of paying attention to the commonplace details of the lives of otherwise forgettable ordinary people, and particularly people below one's own social level, with whom one would not normally be acquainted. It is in the same way that in the late nineteenth century, anthropologists went off to the Torres Straits, and actually engaged for the first time, face to face, with what were previously called 'savages'. And they began to ask for the first time, 'What do they do? How do they cook? How do they get up in the morning? Who is it they feel they can marry, and who is it they feel they can't?' and so on. So probably from the middle of the nineteenth century, when Mayhew did his pioneering interviews, and with accelerating frequency, you get an attention to 'The Other', which epitomises the neglected world of the previously inconsiderable.

Of course, we have to be careful about interpreting what Mayhew reports as being what people might have said to their own friends or relatives. The very nature of these interviews, with someone who is there to give a confession or a discourse about themselves to someone who is recognisably of a different class, and possibly superior, may in fact yield a different type of discourse from the one which Mayhew, instead of hearing, might merely have overheard. For example, there is a great difference between being a 'looker' and being an 'onlooker', and in exactly the same way for speech there may be all the difference in the world between being a listener and an overhearer.

But the important thing is that this doesn't in any way compromise or vitiate the value because these interviews are, in fact, straightforward descriptive accounts of what it is like to be *someone like that*. The philosopher Tom Nagel in a famous paper, asks, 'What is it like to be a bat?'* Now, of course, when it comes to bats, as Nagel says, there is no way in which any interview will yield what it is like to be a bat, and for most people before Mayhew there was no interest in what it was like to be a crossing-sweeper. They may even have been assumed to be not all that different from bats.

What is noticeable about Mayhew, first of all, is that he addresses himself to people who are conspicuously unfortunate, in comparison with someone solvent and respectable like himself, and of a social class which is self-respecting. He addresses, and listens to, people who are quite clearly unfortunate, whose daily work would have been regarded by someone like himself as unconvivial and humiliating. Many of the occupations he explores and analyses are activities which someone of his class would have regarded as quite impossible to engage in, unless one dropped off the edge of one's social class due to drunkenness, or suffered a sudden misfortune which precipitated a slide into this subterranean world.

Indeed, there are a few interviews with such people who were from a social class nearer to Mayhew's own, such as the Seller of Fruity Drinks (p. 18), who was driven into poverty by illness. Such people maintain the language which they learnt of their previous class, and retain fluency and eloquence so that they talk with an accent conspicuously unlike the accents and idioms of the ordinary people, with whom most literate people were unacquainted. It may be that the more elevated language they used, particularly when addressed by someone of their own previous class, helped to maintain their dignity by maintaining the diction of their previous occupation or previous level of occupation.

* *The Philosophical Review* LXXXIII, 4 (October 1974): 435–50

Mayhew described the London he explored as 'the undiscovered country of the poor', and to our shame that country still exists today, and it is still undiscovered by many of us.

When I go down into the nearby market every day to buy fruit or vegetables there are many people in the market with whom I have often quite lengthy conversations, which, if they were written down, would be not altogether different from Mayhew's. They are people from what would have been the same social class as his interviewees. They are none of them, with one or two exceptions, so unfortunate. Nevertheless, right around the corner from where I live there is huge overcrowded residence for the homeless called Arlington House and many of the people there are in situations comparable to those that were reproduced by Mayhew 160 years ago.

But of course, in addition to the poverty endured by the people Mayhew spoke to, there was for some an additional burden of ill-health, reflected in the selection in this book, and one of the interesting things about the representation of the disabled, or the sick, or the ill, is that it is very hard with hindsight, even with some sort of medical knowledge which I still have, actually to make a retrospective diagnosis. I would hesitate to identify any of the disabilities other than by their signs or symptoms, by saying they were blind or lame, or so forth. For example, the Blind Street-reader (p. 101) refers to having had an aneurysm, but what would he know of 'aneurysms'? I suspect that what happened is that he was probably given a diagnosis in the hospital, and hung on to that word, 'aneurysm', without the faintest idea that an aneurysm is in fact a vascular disorder, a sudden dilatation, shortly perhaps to burst, with, perhaps, neurological consequences if it happened to occur inside the skull. Mind you, patients visiting a hospital today often don't have much more understanding of the terms used unless their doctor is a very good communicator. But at least today's doctor will know a lot more about aneurysms and how they cause illness than his Victorian predecessor would have.

For anyone looking at the history of illness through the Mayhew interviews, medical knowledge among doctors, let alone patients, at the time was so rudimentary that it is unlikely that anything the Londoners said to Mayhew about the nature or origins of their condition could be taken at face value. Take the Crippled Seller of Nutmeg-graters, (p. 47) one of the most vivid and moving interviews in the book. As a best guess, he could have had cerebral palsy or some sort of disorder somewhere in the central nervous system that produced difficulties of locomotion which then deteriorated with the effort and difficulty of walking or getting himself around. On the other hand, perhaps he had multiple sclerosis, a disease which itself progresses. But there's no way of knowing – the understanding of diagnostic entities in the middle of the nineteenth century was extremely primitive.

For a long time, there had been some understanding of the organs in the body, based usually on post-mortems. Organs are identifiable because they are lumps which you can see when you open the chest or the abdomen. You can see a blocked intestine; you can see that the heart has undergone some sort of change of colouration, and so on. But it's only when you start doing microscopic analysis of sections of organs that you get to the next level down, what's called histology, the study of tissues. Aniline dyes enabled researchers to stain sections of organs and produce histological diagnoses. It's very interesting that the notion of tissue is derived from 'textile'; it means the same thing, a woven fabric. So up to the eighteenth century you have the notion of 'organs', then you get 'tissues', and then you get 'cells', and you realise that tissues are themselves composed of different types of cells, which then combine in very complicated ways to make the various organs of the body.

Now, at the time when Mayhew is interviewing these people, while biological research was beginning the process of understanding how the body works, the practice of medicine had not yet reached the level of sophistication which enabled anyone to make a useful diagnosis.

Some of the street people give accounts of hospitals and doctors but it is sometimes difficult to tell from the interviews what purpose they served. The Hot-eel Man, for example, (p. 86) stayed in several hospitals for an unconscionably long time. He was in King's College Hospital, St Bartholomew's and the Middlesex for a total of twenty-seven months and I wonder why on earth he was there for so long, how was he treated, and indeed why was he eventually then kicked out? Was it because the doctors said 'We can't do anything more for you'? It's not as if they were doing anything for him anyway.

Of course, hospitals at least provided a sheltered residence with, in some cases, the possibility of surgical interventions – amputations, for example, performed without anaesthetic. Even in the early days of anaesthesia there were no palliative measures, techniques which *reduced* pain as opposed to eliminating it completely during an operation.

Nowadays, many of the most important disease prevention methods spring from an understanding of public health, but in Mayhew's time such understanding barely existed. The early Victorians were on the verge of developing the idea that something was wrong with sewage. There were intimations that ill-health might have been due to the bad arrangement of cities, and 'bad air', what were called miasmas, and even malnutrition. But these causes were not visualised as disorders which you could systematise and classify. No one really thought about what constitutes a healthy diet. That idea developed towards the end of the nineteenth century when there arose an interest in the nature of diet, and the roles of proteins versus carbohydrates. Vitamins were not discovered until the early part of the twentieth century. No one really understood that vitamin deficiency might be the cause of several disorders.

As a result, many of the people Mayhew saw in the streets of London would have had problems of growth or development. They would have been wizened or shrunken. Children would have had various skeletal disorders as a result of inadequate calcium intake, and vitamin D deficiency as a result of poor exposure to sunlight. Scarcity of fruit and vegetables meant a lack of vitamin C. There was no idea of there being components which were necessary to supplement the diet and which people now buy in supermarkets – none of those dietary supplements would have existed because there wasn't a natural history of diet. Mayhew was in no position to ask dietary questions because he himself knew nothing about dietary sufficiency; the biochemistry of diet was something with which he, and everyone else, was unacquainted.

This lack of knowledge of practical measures to prevent or treat disease meant that some of the people Mayhew met had to endure much more advanced stages of illness and disability than any modern patient while still trying to earn a living.

Someone today who had become afflicted in childhood by whatever the Nutmeg-grater Seller had, for example, would probably never have got to the stage of locomotor disorder of Mayhew's interviewee. Many of the cases of profound, almost unintelligible, disorders which figure in Mayhew would not now occur at all. They can be pre-empted, by antenatal care, for example, which did not actually appear as a systematic format until the establishment of the National Health Service, or by pre-natal diagnosis, or intra-uterine surgery, or methods of treatment of babies and young children that were not available in Mayhew's time.

There is a very interesting study of the types of birth disorders that occurred in Scotland among working-class women of the 1940s as the result of an increased frequency of bad deliveries. It turned out that poor women giving birth had had their pelvises affected by malnutrition in *their* infancy, which produced pelvic narrowing, meaning that the birth of their foetuses was compromised; this was not discovered until 1948.

In the absence of such knowledge of cause and effect, people accepted that life was little more than a gamble in which the poor suffered more than did the affluent. Nevertheless, the affluent realised that they would lose many of their children in the first eight years of life. If you look at gravestones from the eighteenth and early nineteenth centuries, you will see how many of those buried are less than four weeks old. Many of them died of diseases for which they would now merely be excused P.E.

Judging from the number of blind people Mayhew spoke to there was a lot more blindness around, or at least, more blind people were forced to work in some capacity. For many, such disability would have been the result of serious infection, preventable today, which would have produced severe scarring on the anterior part of the eyeball, causing opacity of the cornea preventing the retina from receiving a projected image. Few of them wonder about what it would be like to see; perhaps expectations of good fortune are so low that they settle for the misfortunes they been dealt, and are therefore disinclined to wonder about what it is they have lost, and consider this loss as part of the risk of being alive. One might consider this is a kind of stoicism, but I do not think that is accurate in this context. Stoicism is a word you might use of someone who has high expectations of a long and healthy life and is then struck by misfortune, but in a world before effective medical intervention people accepted unaccountable biological misfortunes. There might have been grief, but people settled for their lot. Indeed, they even thanked God that things were not worse.

It may well be that in that period mere survival of self, albeit a reduced form of selfhood, would itself be a privilege, which you would assign to the benevolence of the Creator, notwithstanding the idea that the misfortune itself was the result of the Creator. They saw the Creator as the source of good fortune, and not of bad fortune, and offered praise for the extent to which they survived.

Perhaps this was peculiar to the class to which Mayhew addressed himself. The people he met don't seem to ask the more general question, 'Why am I socially unfortunate?', in addition to 'Why am I medically unfortunate?' There is some sort of acceptance because social structure had not yet been called into question in England. If you read, in Chapter 3, the conversations Mayhew had with the crossing-sweepers, there seems to be no question of resentment of their social position as they make a path for the affluent, stepping delicately through the mud and the shit. They don't ask, 'Why is it that I am sweeping for them, and that no one is sweeping for me? Why is the social structure organised such that I have, in addition to my medical disorder, a social disorder which assigns me to a job which I know these gentry would regard as an impossible humiliation?'

They may have seen what the gentry looked like when they crossed the road, but could not conceive of the gentry's lives when they had crossed the road and returned to their homes, and what their occupations were which made them relatively immune to injuries suffered by those on a lower social level.

One of the things that is most conspicuous about these interviews is that there is little social indignation, and, as a consequence, little sense of social injustice. There is no apparent expression of 'It is unfair'. Social discrepancy was not yet articulated and visualised in ways which gave rise to socially organised discontent. Only then would revolutions begin to occur, or at least social organisations arise which through unions and other organisations could express the notion of injustice.

This is partly lack of information, but also lack of rhetoric. Where does the rhetoric start to spread which gives the working class the sense that there is an articulated justification for discontent? And it isn't just that they are quietly forbearing, there is not yet a language in which the notion of injustice and discontent come together and express themselves in some sort of social arrangement of outrage.

It may of course be that Mayhew avoided raising those issues, because in fact, being of the class that he was, he did not wish to open the lid to the notion of unfairness, either the unfairness on the part of the Creator, or the unfairness on the part of 'my betters'.

It is one result of the neutrality with which Mayhew went about his task that *we* can ask these questions, and many others, on behalf of his interviewees when, on the whole, he does not. He was the earliest 'fly on the wall' journalist, and it is thanks to the fact that he provides such a wealth of raw data about poor people's working lives that his interviews, of which this book contains merely a small selection, are such a fertile stimulus for speculation, curiosity and wonder.

– *Jonathan Miller, 2011*

A note on the text

For many readers who approach Henry Mayhew's daunting four-volume work, *London Labour and the London Poor,* the principal reward is the eye-opening verbatim transcripts of the interviews Mayhew carried out in the streets of London in the middle of the nineteenth century. At the time, they were the earliest printed examples of how 'ordinary people' spoke, and conveyed both the words and expressions they used and the topics that preoccupied them.

The novelist, William Makepeace Thackeray, was bowled over by what Mayhew had produced, when his writings were first published in the *Morning Chronicle*:

> [H]e goes amongst labouring people and poor of all kinds and brings back what? A picture of human life so wonderful, so awful, so piteous and pathetic, so exciting and terrible, that readers of romances own they never read anything like to it; and that the griefs, struggles, strange adventures here depicted exceed anything that any of us could imagine... We have hitherto had no community with the poor. We never speak a word to the servant who waits on us for twenty years; we condescend to employ a tradesman, keeping him at a proper distance...; of his workmen we know nothing, how pitilessly they are ground down, how they live and die, here close by us at the backs of our houses; until... some clear-sighted, energetic man like the writer of the *Chronicle* travels into the poor man's country for us, and comes back with his tale of terror and wonder.

For Mayhew, the interviews were part of a greater work – an analysis of the economy of the street people. Mayhew hoped that at a time of increasing mechanisation and the use of sweated labour he could gain some insights into the relation-ships between employer and employee, customer and trades-man, as applied to the poorest people in Britain's largest city. But the theories and analyses that form the framework of his book have become outdated. We no longer need to worry, as Mayhew did, about the vast quantities of horse manure that would eventually overwhelm London's streets as passenger traffic grew.

Far more enduring and significant have been the voices of Victorian Londoners as scattered in a fairly undisciplined way through Mayhew's text. For the purpose of this book, a selection of the five hundred or so interviews Mayhew pub-lished has been isolated from the narrative text and presented in an arrangement that highlights one of the many topics that crept into the interviews even when Mayhew did not start out with the particular topic in mind. This particular selection deals with accounts of the burden of ill-health and disability that often crept into people's conversations with Mayhew, and Jonathan Miller writes in his introduction about the limits of medical knowledge, the paucity of available remedial measures, and the extraordinary forbearance of people who not only had to put up with more pain and discomfort than most people do today, but actually had to earn a living in the midst of their suffering.

But these interviews contain much more. Although his main purpose was an understanding of the economics of street life, Mayhew's approach was so undisciplined – or perhaps he himself was so fascinated – that he allowed his interviewees to tell him about anything and everything, and he or his hired stenographers took it all down.

Mayhew seems to have made little attempt to stem the flow when people embarked on a topic they wanted to talk about even if it didn't fit Mayhew's agenda. The Poorly Poet tells us about his abscesses but he also recites some of his poetry to Mayhew, and it is only near the end of the interview that the poet gives Mayhew the financial information he professes to be interested in.

Minor changes in spelling and punctuation have been made and where Mayhew left a blank for a name of a person or place one has been made up for ease of reading. The interviews are taken from the first three volumes of the 1861–2 edition, and the source for each interview is given at the back of the book.

– Karl Sabbagh

Voices of Victorian London

Chapter One: The Public Health

In the days before antisepsis, antibiotics, or even a general sense of the causes of major infections, the burden of disease from bad air, bad water, and bad food hygiene was huge. Many of Mayhew's interviewees had suffered from the major scourge of cholera, not traced to poor water supplies until John Snow's analysis which connected the pattern of deaths from an outbreak of the disease in Soho in 1854 to the output of one waterpump in Broad Street.

Staphylococcal infections – boils, blood poisoning, infected wounds – and contagious diseases faced little resistance and no treatment or cure. There was, however, a dim recognition that flies, rats and other vermin might be harmful to health, and sellers of fly-paper and catchers of rats could earn a decent living as a result.

A Fly-paper Seller

Fly-papers came, generally, into street-traffic, I am informed, in the summer of 1848. The fly-papers are sold wholesale at many of the oil-shops, but the principal shop for the supply of the street-traders is in Whitechapel. The wholesale price is twopence farthing a dozen, and the (street) retail charge a halfpenny a paper, or three for a penny. A young man, to whom I was referred, and whom I found selling, or rather bartering, crockery, gave me the following account of his experience of the fly-paper trade. He was a rosy-cheeked, strong-built young fellow, and said he thought he was 'getting on' in his present trade. He spoke merrily of his troubles, as I have found common among his class, when they are over:–

I went into the fly-paper trade – it's nearly two years ago, I think – because a boy I slept with did tidy in it. We bought the papers at the first shop as was open, and then got leave of the deputy of the lodging house to catch all the flies we could, and we stuck them thick on the paper, and fastened the paper to our hats. I used to think, when I was in service, how a smart livery hat, with a cockade to it, would look, but instead of that I turned out, the first time in my life that ever I sold anything, with my hat stuck round with flies. I felt so ashamed I could have cried. I was miserable, I felt so awkward. But I spent my last twopence in some gin and milk to give me courage, and that brightened me up a bit, and I set to work. I went Mile End way, and got out of the main streets, and I suppose I'd gone into streets and places where there hadn't often been fly-papers before, and I soon had a lot of boys following me, and I felt, almost, as if I'd picked a pocket, or done something to be 'shamed of. I could hardly cry 'Catch 'em alive, only a halfpenny!' But I found I could sell my papers to public-houses and shopkeepers, such as grocers and confectioners, and that gave me pluck. The boys caught flies, and then came up to me, and threw them against my hat, and if they stuck the lads set up a shout. I stuck to the trade, however, and took two and sixpence to three shillings every day that week, more than half of it profit, and on Saturday I took five and sixpence.

The trade is all to housekeepers. I called at open shops and looked up at the windows, or held up my hat at private houses, and was sometimes beckoned to go in and sell my papers. Women bought most, I think. 'Nasty things,' they used to say, 'there's no keeping nothing clean for them'.

Some of the fly-paper sellers make their stock-in-trade, but three-fourths of the number buy them ready-made. The street-sellers make them of old newspapers or other waste-paper, no matter how dirty. To the paper they apply turpentine and common coach varnish, some using resin instead of varnish, and occasionally they dash a few grains of sugar over the composition when spread upon the paper.

Last summer, I was informed, there were fifty or sixty persons selling fly-papers and beetle wafers in the streets; some of them boys, and all of them of the general class of street-sellers, who 'take' to any trade for which a shilling suffices as capital. Their average earnings may be estimated at two and sixpence a day, about one-half being profit. This gives a street outlay, say for a 'season' of ten weeks, of £375 calculating fifty sellers. A few of these street traders carried a side of a newspaper, black with flies, attached to a stick, waving it like a flag. The cries were 'Catch 'em alive! Catch 'em alive for one shilling and twopence!' 'New method of destroying thousands!'[1]

One lad I spoke to was of a middle age, and although the noisiest when among his companions, had no sooner entered the room with me, than his whole manner changed. He sat himself down, bent up like a monkey, and scarcely ever turned his eyes from me. He seemed as nervous as if in a witness-box, and kept playing with his grubby fingers till he had almost made them white.

They calls me 'Curley'. I come from Ireland. I'm about fourteen year, and have been in this line now, sir, about five year. I goes about the borders of the country. We general takes up the line about the beginning of June, that is, when we gets a good summer. When we gets a good close dull day like this, we does pretty well, but when we has first one day hot, and then another rainy and could, a' course we don't get on so well.

The most I sold was one day when I went to Uxbridge, and then I sold a gross and a half. I paid half-a-crown a gross for

5

them. I was living with mother then, and she give me the money to buy 'em, but I had to bring her back again all as I took. I al'us give her all I makes, except sixpence as I wants for my dinner, which is a kipple of pen'orth of bread and cheese and a pint of beer. I sold that gross and a half I spoke on at a ha'penny each, and I took nine shillings, so that I made five and sixpence. But then I'd to leave London at three or four o'clock in the morning, and to stop out till twelve o'clock at night. I used to live out at Hammersmith then, and come up to St Giles's every morning and buy the papers. I had to rise by half-past two in the morning, and I'd get back again to Hammersmith by about six o'clock. I couldn't sill none on the road, 'cos the shops wasn't open.

The flies is getting bad every summer. This year they a'n't half so good as they was last year or the year before. I'm sure I don't know why there ain't so many, but they ain't so plentiful like. The best year was three year ago. I know that by the quantity as my customers bought of me, and in three days the papers was swarmed with flies.

I've got regular customers, where I calls two or three times a week to 'em. If I was to walk my rounds over I could at the lowest sell from six to eight dozen at ha'penny each at wonst. If it was nice weather, like to-day, so that it wouldn't come wet on me, I should make ten shillings a week regular, but it depends on the weather. If I was to put my profits by, I'm sure I should find I make more than six shillings a week, and nearer eight. But the season is only for three months at most, and then we takes to boot-cleaning. Near all the poor boys about here is fly-paper selling in the hot weather, and boot-cleaners at other times.

Shops buys the most of us in London. In Barnet I sell sometimes as much as six or seven dozen to some of the grocers as buys to sell again, but I don't let them have them only when

I can't get rid of 'em to t'other customers. Butchers is very fond of the papers, to catch the blue-bottles as gets in their meat, though there is a few butchers as have said to me, 'Oh, go away, they draws the flies more than they ketches 'em.' Clothes-shops, again, is very fond of 'em. I can't tell why they is fond of 'em, but I suppose 'cos the flies spots the goods.

There's lots of boys going selling 'ketch 'em alive oh's' from Golden Lane, and Whitechapel, and the Borough. There's lots, too, comes out of Gray's Inn Lane and St Giles's. Near every boy who has nothing to do goes out with fly-papers. Perhaps it ain't that the flies is falled off that we don't sell so many papers now, but because there's so many boys at it.[2]

Rats and their Catchers

The proprietor of one of the largest sporting public-houses in London, who is celebrated for the rat-matches which come off weekly at his establishment, was kind enough to favour me with a few details as to the quality of those animals which are destroyed in his pit. His statement was certainly one of the most curious that I have listened to, and it was given to me with a readiness and a courtesy of manner such as I have not often met with during my researches. The landlord himself is known in pugilistic circles as one of the most skilful boxers among what is termed the 'light weights'.

His statement is curious, as a proof of the large trade which is carried on in these animals, for it would seem that the men who make a business of catching rats are not always employed as 'exterminators', for they make a good living as 'purveyors' for supplying the demands of the sporting portion of London.

'The poor people,' said the sporting landlord, 'who supply me with rats, are what you may call barn-door labouring poor, for they are the most ignorant people I ever come near. Really you would not believe people could live in such ignorance. Talk about Latin and Greek, sir, why English is Latin to them – in fact, I have a difficulty to understand them myself.'

Enfield is a kind of head-quarters for rat-ketchers. It's dangerous work, though, for you see there is a wonderful deal of difference in the specie of rats. The bite of sewer or waterditch rats is very bad. The water and ditch rat lives on filth, but your barn-rat is a plump fellow, and he lives on the best of everything. He's well off. There's as much difference between the barn and sewer-rats as between a brewer's horse and a costermonger's. Sewer rats are very bad for dogs, their coats is poisonous.

Some of the rats that are brought to me are caught in the warehouses in the City. Wherever there is anything in the shape of provisions, there you are sure to find Mr Rat an intruder. The ketchers are paid for ketching them in the warehouses, and then they are sold to me as well, so the men must make a good thing of it. Many of the more courageous kind of warehousemen will take a pleasure in hunting the rats themselves.

I should think I buy in the course of the year, on the average, from 300 to 700 rats a-week. [Taking 500 as the weekly average, this gives a yearly purchase of 26,000 live rats.] That's what I kill taking all the year round, you see. Some first-class chaps will come here in the day-time, and they'll try their dogs. They'll say, 'Jimmy, give the dog 100.' After he's polished them off they'll say, perhaps, 'Hang it, give him another 100.'

'Bless you!' he added, in a kind of whisper, 'I've had noble ladies and titled ladies come here to see the sport – on the quiet, you know. When my wife was here they would come regular, but now she's away they don't come so often.'

The largest quantity of rats I've bought from one man was five guineas' worth, or thirty-five dozen at threepence a head, and that's a load for a horse. This man comes up from Clavering in a kind of cart, with a horse that's a regular phenomena, for it ain't like a beast nor nothing. I pays him a good deal of money at times, and I'm sure I can't tell what he does with it; but they do tell me that he deals in old iron, and goes buying it up, though he don't seem to have much of a head-piece for that sort of fancy neither.

I've had as many as 2,000 rats in this very house at one time. They'll consume a sack of barley-meal a week, and the brutes, if you don't give 'em good stuff, they'll eat one another, hang 'em!... Have I been bit by them? Aye, hundreds of times. Now, some people will say, 'Rub yourself over with caraway and stuff, and then rats won't bite you.' But I give you my word and honour it's all nonsense, sir. Bless you, there's nothing that a rat won't bite through. I've seen my lads standing in the pit with the rats running about them, and if they haven't taken the precaution to tie their trousers round with a bit of string at the bottom, they'd have as many as five or six rats run up their trouser-legs. They'll deliberately take off their clothes and pick them out from their shirts, and bosoms, and breeches. Some people is amused, and others is horror-struck. People have asked them whether they ain't rubbed? They'll say 'Yes,' but that's as a lark; 'cos, sometimes when my boy has been taking the rats out of the cage, and somebody has taken his attention off, talking to him, he has had a bite, and will turn to me with his finger bleeding, and say, 'Yes, I'm rubbed, ain't I, father? look here!'

A rat's bite is very singular, it's a threecornered one, like a leech's, only deeper, of course, and it will bleed for ever such a time. My boys have sometimes had their fingers go dreadfully bad from rat-bites, so that they turn all black and putrid like – aye, as black as the horse-hair covering to my sofa. People have said to me, 'You ought to send the lad to the hospital, and have his finger took off', but I've always left it to the lads, and they've said, 'Oh, don't mind it, father; it'll get all right by and by.' And so it has.

The best thing I ever found for a rat-bite was the thick bottoms of porter casks put on as a poultice. The only thing you can do is to poultice, and these porter bottoms is so powerful and draws so, that they'll actually take thorns out of horses' hoofs and feet after steeplechasing.

In handling rats, it's nothing more in the world but nerve that does it. I should faint now if a rat was to run up my breeches, but I have known the time when I've been kivered with 'em.

I generally throw my dead rats away now; but two or three years since my boys took the idea of skinning them into their heads, and they did about 300 of them, and their skins was very promising. The boys was, after all, obliged to give them away to a furrier, for my wife didn't like the notion, and I said, 'Throw them away;' but the idea strikes me to be something, and one that is lost sight of, for the skins are warm and handsome-looking – a beautiful grey.

There's nothing turns so quickly as dead rats, so I am obliged to have my dustmen come round every Wednesday morning; and regularly enough they call too, for they know where there is a bob and a pot. I generally prefers using the authorised dustmen, though the others come sometimes – the flying dustmen they call 'em – and if they're first, they has the job.

It strikes me, though, that to throw away so many valuable skins is a good thing lost sight of.

The rats want a deal of watching, and a deal of sorting. Now you can't put a sewer and a barn-rat together, it's like putting a Rooshian and a Turk under the same roof.

I can tell a barn-rat from a ship-rat or a sewer-rat in a minute, and I have to look over my stock when they come in, or they'd fight to the death. There's six or seven different kinds of rats, and if we don't sort 'em they tear one another to pieces. I think when I have a number of rats in the house, that I am a lucky man if I don't find a dozen dead when I go up to them in the morning; and when I tell you that at times – when I've wanted to make up my number for a match – I've given twenty one shillings for twenty rats, you may think I lose something that way every year. Rats, even now, is occasionally six shillings a dozen; but that, I think, is most inconsistent.

If I had my will, I wouldn't allow sewer ratting, for the rats in the shores eats up a great quantity of sewer filth and rubbish, and is another specie of scavenger in their own way.[3]

About that time a troop of rats flew at the feet of another of my informants, and would no doubt have maimed him seriously, 'but my boots,' said he, 'stopped the devils'. 'The sewers generally swarms with rats,' said another man. 'I runs away from 'em; I don't like 'em. They in general gets away from us; but in case we comes to a stunt end where there's a wall and no place for 'em to get away, and we goes to touch 'em, they fly at us. They're some of 'em as big as good-sized kittens. One of our men caught hold of one the other day by the tail, and he found it trying to release itself, and the tail slipping through his fingers; so he put up his left hand to stop it, and the rat caught hold of his finger, and the man's got an arm now as big as his thigh.'

I heard from several that there had been occasionally battles among the rats, one with another.[4]

A Poorly Poet

I found the poor poet, who bears a good character, on a sick bed; he was suffering, and had long been suffering, from abscesses. He was apparently about forty-five, with the sunken eyes, hollow cheeks, and, not pale but thick and rather sallow complexion, which indicate ill-health and scant food. He spoke quietly, and expressed resignation. His room was not very small, and was furnished in the way usual among the very poor, but there were a few old pictures over the mantel-piece. His eldest boy, a lad of thirteen or fourteen, was making dog-chains; at which he earned a shilling or two, sometimes two and sixpence by sale in the streets.

'I was born at Newcastle-under-Lyne,' the man said,

but was brought to London when, I believe, I was only three months old. I was very fond of reading poems, in my youth, as soon as I could read and understand almost. I was taught wire-working, and jobbing, and was brought up to hawking wire-work in the streets, and all over England and Wales. It was never a very good trade, just a living. Many and many a weary mile we've travelled together – I mean, my wife and I have: and we've sometimes been benighted, and had to wander or rest about until morning. It wasn't that we hadn't money to pay for a lodging, but we couldn't get one. We lost count of the days sometimes in wild parts; but if we did lose count, or thought we had, I could always tell when it was Sunday morning by the look of nature; there was a mystery and a beauty about it as told me. I was very

fond of Goldsmith's poetry always. I can repeat 'Edwin and Emma' now. No, sir; I never read the 'Vicar of Wakefield'. I found 'Edwin and Emma' in a book called the 'Speaker'. I often thought of it in travelling through some parts of the country.

Above fourteen years ago I tried to make a shilling or two by selling my verses. I'd written plenty before, but made nothing by them. Indeed I never tried. The first song I ever sold was to a concert-room manager. The next I sold had great success. It was called the 'Demon of the Sea', and was to the tune of 'The Brave Old Oak'. Do I remember how it began? Yes, sir, I remember every word of it. It began:

Unfurl the sails,
We've easy gales;
And helmsman steer aright,
Hoist the grim death's head –
The Pirate's head –
For a vessel heaves in sight!

That song was written for a concert-room, but it was soon in the streets, and ran a whole winter. I got only a shilling for it. Then I wrote the 'Pirate of the Isles', and other ballads of that sort. The concert-rooms pay no better than the printers for the streets.

Perhaps the best thing I ever wrote was the 'Husband's Dream'. I'm very sorry indeed that I can't offer you copies of some of my ballads, but I haven't a single copy myself of any of them, not one, and I dare say I've written a thousand in my time, and most of them were printed. I believe 10,000 were sold of the 'Husband's Dream'. It begins:

O Dermot, you look healthy now,
Your dress is neat and clean;
I never see you drunk about,
Then tell me where you've been.
Your wife and family – are they well?
You once did use them strange:
O, are you kinder to them grown,
How came this happy change?

Then Dermot tells how he dreamed of his wife's sudden death, and his children's misery as they cried about her dead body, while he was drunk in bed, and as he calls out in his misery, he wakes, and finds his wife by his side. The ballad ends:

I pressed her to my throbbing heart,
Whilst joyous tears did stream;
And ever since, I've heaven blest,
For sending me that dream.

Dermot turned teetotaller. The teetotallers were very much pleased with that song. The printer once sent me five shillings on account of it.

I have written all sorts of things – ballads on a subject, and copies of verses, and anything ordered of me, or on anything I thought would be accepted, but now I can't get about. I've been asked to write indecent songs, but I refused. One man offered me 5s. for six such songs. 'Why, that's less than the common price,' said I, 'instead of something over to pay for the wickedness'. All those sort of songs come now to the streets, I believe all do, from the concert-rooms.

Writing poetry is no comfort to me in my sickness. It might if I could write just what I please. The printers like hanging subjects best, and I don't. But when any of them sends to order a copy of verses for a 'Sorrowful Lamentation' of course I must supply them. I don't think much of what I've done that way. If I'd my own fancy, I'd keep writing acrostics, such as one I wrote on our rector.

'God bless him,' interrupted the wife, 'he's a good man'.

'That he is,' said the poet, 'but he's never seen what I wrote about him, and perhaps never will'. He then desired his wife to reach him his big Bible, and out of it he handed me a piece of paper, with the following lines written on it, in a small neat hand enough:

C elestial blessings hover round his head,
H undreds of poor, by his kindness were fed,
A nd precepts taught which he himself obeyed.
M an, erring man, brought to the fold of God,
P reaching pardon through a Saviour's blood.
N o lukewarm priest, but firm to Heaven's cause;
E xamples showed how much he loved its laws.
Y outh and age, he to their wants attends,
S teward of Christ -the poor man's sterling friend.

'There would be some comfort, sir,' he continued,

if one could go on writing at will like that. As it is, I some-times write verses all over a slate, and rub them out again. Indeed, we do live hard. I hardly know the taste of meat. We live on bread and butter, and tea; no, not any fish. As you see, sir, I work at tinning. I put new bottoms into old tin tea-pots, and such like. Here's my sort of bench, by my poor bit of a bed. In the best weeks I earn four shillings by tinning, never higher. In bad weeks I earn only one shilling by it, and sometimes not that – and there are more shilling than four shilling weeks by three to one. As to my poetry, a good week is three shillings and a poor week is a shilling – and sometimes I make nothing at all that way. So I leave you to judge, sir, whether we live hard; for the comings in, and what we have from the parish, must keep six of us – myself, my wife, and four children. It's a long, hard struggle.

'Yes, indeed,' said the wife, 'it's just as you've heard my husband tell, sir. We've two shillings a week and four loaves of bread from the parish, and the rent's two and sixpence, and the landlord every week has two shillings, – and sixpence he has done for him in tinning work. Oh, we do live hard, indeed.'

As I was taking my leave, the poor man expressed a desire that I would take a copy of an epitaph which he had written for himself. 'If ever,' he said, 'I am rich enough to provide for a tomb-stone, or my family is rich enough to give me one, this shall be my epitaph.'

[I copied it from a blank page in his Bible:]
Stranger, pause, a moment stay,
Tread lightly o'er this mound of clay.
Here lies John Hart, in hopes to rise,
And meet his Saviour in the skies.
Christ his refuge,
Heaven his home,
Where pain and sorrow never come.
His journey's done, his trouble's past,
With God he sleeps in peace at last.

A Seller of Fruity Drinks

He was an intelligent-looking man, of about thirty-five, but with nothing very particular in his appearance unless it were a head of very curly hair. He gave me the statement in his own room, which was larger than I have usually found such abodes, and would have been very bare, but that it was somewhat littered with the vessels of his trade as a street-seller of Nectar, Persian Sherbet, Raspberryade, and other decoctions of coloured ginger-beer, with high-sounding names and indifferent flavour: in the summer he said he could live better thereby, with a little costering, than by street-sweeping, but being often a sickly man he could not do so during the uncertainties of a winter street trade. His wife, a decent looking woman, was present occasionally, suckling one child, about two years old – for the poor often protract the weaning of their children, as the mother's nutriment is the *cheapest* of all food for the infant, and as the means of postponing the further increase of their family – whilst another of five or six years of age sat on a bench by her side. There was nothing on the walls in the way of an ornament, as I have seen in some of the rooms of the poor, for the couple had once been in the workhouse, and might be driven there again, and with such apprehensions did not care, perhaps, to make a home otherwise than they found it, even if the consumption of only a little spare time were involved. The husband said:

I was brought up as a type-founder; my father, who was one, learnt me his trade; but he died when I was quite a young man, or I might have been better perfected in it. I was comfortably off enough then, and got married. Very soon after that I was taken ill with an abscess in my neck, you can see the mark of it still. [He showed me the mark.] For six months I wasn't able to do a thing, and I was a part of the time – I don't recollect how long – in St Bartholomew's Hospital. I was weak and ill when I came out, and hardly fit for work; I couldn't hear of any work I could get, for there was a great bother in the trade between master and men. Before I went into the hospital, there was money to pay to doctors; and when I came out I could earn nothing, so everything went, yes, sir, everything. My wife made a little matter with charring for families she'd lived in, but things are in a bad way if a poor woman has to keep her husband. She was taken ill at last, and then there was nothing but the parish for us. I suffered a great deal before it come to that. It was awful. No one can know what it is but them that suffers it. But I didn't know what in the world to do. We lived then in St Luke's, and were passed to our own parish, and were three months in the workhouse. The living was good enough, better then than it is now, I've heard, but I was miserable.

'And I was *very* miserable,' interposed the wife, 'for I had been brought up comfortable; my father was a respectable tradesman in St George's-in-the-East, and I had been in good situations.'

'We made ourselves,' said the husband,

as useful as we could, but we were parted of course. At the three months' end, I had ten shillings given to me to come out with, and was told I might start costermongering on it. But to a man not up to the trade, ten shillings won't go very far to keep up costering. I didn't feel master enough of my own trade by this time to try for work at it, and work wasn't at all regular. There were good hands earning only twelve shillings a week. The ten shillings soon went, and I had again to apply for relief, and got an order for the stone-yard to go and break stones. Ten bushels was to be broken for fifteen pence. It was dreadful hard work at first. My hands got all blistered and bloody, and I've gone home and cried with pain and wretchedness. At first it was on to three days before I could break the ten bushels. I felt shivered to bits all over my arms and shoulders, and my head was splitting. I then got to do it in two days, and then in one, and it grew easier. But all this time I had only what was reckoned three days' work in a week. That is, you see, sir, I had only three times ten bushels of stones given to break in the week, and earned only three shillings and ninepence. I lived on it, and paid one shilling sixpence a week rent, for the neighbours took care of a few sticks for us, and the parish or a broker wouldn't have found them worth carriage. My wife was then in the country with a sister. I lived upon bread and dripping, went without fire or candle (or had one only very seldom) though it wasn't warm weather. I can safely say that for eight weeks I never tasted one bite of meat, and hardly a bite of butter. When I couldn't sleep of a night, but that wasn't often, it was terrible, very. I washed what bits of things I had then myself, and had sometimes to get a ha'porth of soap as a favour, as the chandler said she 'didn't make less than a penn'orth'. If I eat too much dripping, it made me feel sick. I hardly know how much bread and dripping I eat in a week. I spent what money I had in it and bread, and sometimes went without. I was very weak, you may be sure, sir; and if I'd had the influenza or anything that way, I should have gone off like a shot, for I seemed to have no constitution left. But my wife came back again and got work at charing, and made about four shillings a week at it; but we were still very badly off. Then I got to work on the roads every day, and had a shilling and a quartern loaf a day, which was a rise. I had only one child then, but men with larger families got two quartern loaves a day. Single men got ninepence a day. It was far easier work than stone-breaking too. The hours were from eight to five in winter, and from seven to six in summer. But there's always changes going on, and we were put on a shilling and a penny halfpenny a day and a quartern loaf, and only three days a week. All the same as to time of course. The bread wasn't good; it was only cheap. I suppose there was twenty of us working most of the times as I was. The gangsman, as you call him, but that's more for the regular hands, was a servant of the parish, and a great tyrant.[5]

A Shellfish Seller

I had the following account from an experienced man. He lived with his mother, his wife, and four children, in one of the streets near Gray's Inn Lane. The street was inhabited altogether by people of his class, the women looking sharply out when a stranger visited the place. On my first visit to this man's room, his wife, who is near her confinement, was at dinner with her children. The time was a quarter to twelve. The meal was tea, and bread with butter very thinly spread over it. On the wife's bread was a small piece of pickled pork, covering about one-eighth of the slice of a quartern loaf cut through. In one corner of the room, which is on the ground floor, was a scantily-covered bed. A few dingy-looking rags were hanging up to dry in the middle of the room, which was littered with baskets and boxes, mixed up with old furniture, so that it was a difficulty to stir. The room (although the paper, covering the broken panes in the window, was torn and full of holes) was most oppressively close and hot, and there was a fetid smell, difficult to sustain, though it was less noticeable on a subsequent call. I have often had occasion to remark that the poor, especially those who are much subjected to cold in the open air, will sacrifice much

for heat. The adjoining room, which had no door, seemed littered like the one where the family were. The walls of the room I was in were discoloured and weather-stained. The only attempt at ornament was over the mantel-shelf, the wall here being papered with red and other gay-coloured papers, that once had been upholsterer's patterns.

On my second visit, the husband was at dinner with the family, on good boiled beef and potatoes. He was a small-featured man, with a head of very curly and long black hair, and both in mien, manners, and dress, resembled the mechanic far more than the costermonger. He said:

I've been twenty years and more, perhaps twenty-four, selling shell-fish in the streets. I was a boot-closer when I was young, and have made my twenty and thirty shillings, and sometimes forty shillings, and then sometimes not ten shillings a week; but I had an attack of rheumatic fever, and lost the use of my hands for my trade. The streets hadn't any great name, as far as I knew, then, but as I couldn't work, it was just a choice between street-selling and starving, so I didn't prefer the last. It was reckoned degrading to go into the streets but I couldn't help that. I was astonished at my success when I first began, and got into the business – that is into the understanding of it – after a week, or two, or three. Why, I made £3 the first week I knew my trade, properly; yes, I cleared £3! I made, not long after, £5 a week – but not often. I was giddy and extravagant. Indeed, I was a fool, and spent my money like a fool. I could have brought up a family then like a gentleman – I send them to school as it is – but I hadn't a wife and family then, or it might have been better; it's a great check on a man, is a family. I began with shell-fish, and sell it still; very seldom anything else. There's more demand for shells, no doubt, because it's far cheaper, but then there's so many more sellers.

I don't know why exactly. I suppose it's because poor people go into the streets when they can't live other ways, and some do it because they think it's an idle life; but it ain't. Where I took thirty-five shillings in a day at my stall – and well on to half of it profit – I now take five or six shillings, or perhaps seven shillings, in the day and less profit on that less money. I don't clear three shillings a day now, take the year through. I don't keep accounts, but I'm certain enough that I average about fifteen shillings a week the year through, and my wife has to help me to make that. She'll mind the stall, while I take a round sometimes. I sell all kinds of shell-fish, but my great dependence is on winkles. I don't do much in lobsters. Very few speculate in them. The price varies very greatly. What's ten shillings a score one day may be twenty-five shillings the next. I sometimes get a score for five or six shillings, but it's a poor trade, for sixpence is the top of the tree, with me, for a price to a seller. I never get more. I sell them to mechanics and tradesmen. I do more in pound crabs. There's a great call for haporths and pennorths of lobster or crab, by children; that's their claws. I boil them all myself, and buy them alive. I can boil twenty in half an hour, and do it over a grate in a back-yard. Lobsters don't fight or struggle much in the hot water, if they're properly packed. It's very few that knows how to boil a lobster as he should be boiled. I wish I knew any way of killing lobsters before boiling them. I can't kill them without smashing them to bits, and that won't do at all.

I kill my crabs before I boil them. I stick them in the throat with a knife and they're dead in an instant. Some sticks them with a skewer, but they kick a good while with the skewer in them. It's a shame to torture anything when it can be helped. If I didn't kill the crabs they'd shed every leg in the hot water; they'd come out as bare of claws as this plate. I've known it oft enough, as it is; though I kill them uncommon quick, a crab will be quicker and shed every leg – throw them off in the moment I kill them, but that doesn't happen once in fifty times.

Oysters are capital this season, I mean as to quality, but they're not a good sale. I made £3 a week in oysters, not reckoning anything else, eighteen or twenty years back. It was easy to make money then; like putting down one sovereign and taking two up. I sold oysters then oft enough at a penny a piece. Now I sell far finer at three a penny and five for twopence. People can't spend money in shell-fish when they haven't got any. They say that fortune knocks once at every man's door. I wish I'd opened my door when he knocked at it.

This man's wife told me afterwards, that last winter, after an attack of rheumatism, all their stock-money was exhausted, and her husband sat day by day at home almost out of his mind; for nothing could tempt him to apply to the parish, and 'he would never have mentioned his sufferings to me,' she said; 'he had too much pride'. The loan of a few shillings from a poor costermonger enabled the man to go to market again, or he and his family would now have been in the Union.[6]

The sufferings of the costermongers during the prevalence of the cholera in 1849 were intense. Their customers generally relinquished the consumption of potatoes, greens, fruit, and fish; indeed, of almost every article on the consumption of which the costermongers depend for his daily bread. Many were driven to apply to the parish; 'many had relief and many hadn't', I was told. Two young men, within the knowledge of one of my informants, became professional thieves, after enduring much destitution. It does not appear that the costermongers mani-fested any personal dread of the visitation of the cholera, or thought that their lives were imperilled: 'We weren't a bit afraid,' said one of them, and, perhaps, that was the reason so few costers died of the cholera. I knew them all in Lambeth, I think, and I knew only one die of it, and he drank hard. Poor Waxy! He was a good fellow enough, and was well known in the Cut. But it was a terrible time for us, sir. It seems to me now like a shocking dream. Fish I couldn't sell a bit of; the people had a perfect dread of it – all but the poor Irish, and there was no making a crust out of them. *They* had no dread of fish, however; indeed, they reckon it a religious sort of living, living on fish, – but they *will* have it dirt cheap. We were in terrible distress all that time.[7]

A Shoemaker's Widow

The poor woman whom I accosted was a widow (her husband having died only a few months before). She had altogether what I may call a faded look; even her widow's cap was limp and flat, and her look was miserably subdued. She said:–

My husband was a journeyman shoemaker. Sometimes he would earn a pound a week; but we were badly off, for he drank; but he did not ill-use me – not much. During his last illness we raised £5 on a raffle for a silk handkerchief among the shoemakers, and ten shillings from the Mendicity Society, and a few shillings from the clergyman of the parish. The trade buried him. I didn't get a shilling as his widow – only £5 to bury him; but there was arrears of rent to pay, and about a month after his death I hadn't a farthing, and I took the cholera, and was eight days in St Bartholomew's, the parish officers sending me there in a cab. I lived in furnished lodgings before that, and had nothing to call my own, when I had pawned my black for my husband. When I got out

I helped a neighbour at shoe-binding. One time I have earned fifteen shillings a week at shoebinding for Taplow's of Regent Street. Now I can only earn five shillings with full work. I have seldom earned three shillings of late weeks. I had to leave my neighbour, because I felt that I was a burden, and was imposing upon her. I then had a shelter with a young woman I once lodged with, but I couldn't stay there any longer. She was poor, and had nothing for me to do. So, on Saturday last, I had no work, no money, no friends, and I thought I would try and get in here, as another poor woman had done. Here I've had a shelter.[8]

A Soldier's Wife

She had altogether a decent appearance, but her features – and there were the remains of prettiness in her look – were sadly pinched. Her manners were quiet, and her voice low and agreeable. She looked like one who had 'seen better days', as the poor of the better sort not unfrequently say in their destitution, clinging to the recollection of past comforts. She wore a very clean checked cotton shawl, and a straw bonnet tolerably entire. The remainder of her dress was covered by her shawl, which was folded closely about her, over a dark cotton gown.

I was born twenty miles from Inverness [she said] and have been a servant since I was eleven. I always lived in good places – the best of places. I never was in inferior places. I have lived as cook, housemaid, or servant-of-all-work, in Inverness, Elgin, and Tain, always maintaining a good character. I thank God for that. In all my distress I've done nothing wrong, but I didn't know what distress was when in service. I continued in service until I married; but I was not able to save much money, because I had to do all I could for my mother, who was a very poor widow, for I lost my father when I was two years old. Wages are very low in Scotland to what they are in England. In the year 1847 I lived in the service of the barrack-master of Fort George, twelve miles below Inverness. There I became acquainted with my present husband, a soldier, and I was married to him in March, 1847, in the chapel at Fort George. I continued two months in service after my marriage. My mistress wouldn't let me away; she was very kind to me; so was my master: they all were. I have a written character from my mistress. Two months after, the regiment left Fort George for Leith, and there I lived with my husband in barracks. It is not so bad for married persons in the artillery as in the line (we were in the artillery), in barracks. In our barrack-rooms no single men were allowed to sleep where the married people were accommodated. But there were three or four married families in our room. I lived two years in barracks with my husband, in different barracks. I was very comfortable. I didn't know what it was to want anything I ought to have. My husband was a kind, sober man. [This she said very feelingly.] His regiment was ordered abroad, to Nova Scotia. I had no family. Only six soldiers' wives are allowed to go out with each company, and there were seventeen married men in the company to which my husband belonged. It's determined by lot. An officer holds the tickets in his cap, and the men draw them. None of the wives are present. It would be too hard a thing for them to see. My husband drew a blank.

It was a sad scene when they embarked at Woolwich last March. All the wives were there, all crying and sobbing, you may depend upon that; and the children, too, and some of the men; but I couldn't look much at them, and I don't like to see men cry. My husband was sadly distressed. I hoped to get out there and join him, not knowing the passage was so long and expensive. I had a little money then, but that's gone, and I'm brought to misery. It would have cost me £6 at that time to get out, and I couldn't manage that, so I stayed in London, getting a day's work at washing when I could, making a very poor living of it; and I was at last forced to part with all my good clothes after my money went; and my husband, God bless him! always gave me his money to do what I thought best with it. I used to earn a little in barracks with my needle, too. I was taken ill with cholera at the latter end of August. Dear, dear, what I suffered! And when I was getting better I had a second attack, and that was the way my bit of money all went. I was then quite destitute; but I care nothing for that, and would care nothing for anything if I could get out to my husband. I should be happy then. I should never be so happy since I was born before. It's now a month since I was entirely out of halfpence. I can't beg; it would disgrace me and my husband, and I'd die in the streets first. Last Saturday I hadn't a farthing. I hadn't a thing to part with. I had a bed by the night, at threepence a night, not a regular lodging house; but the mistress wouldn't trust me no longer, as I owed her two shillings and sixpence, and for that she holds clothes worth far more than that. I heard of this Asylum, and got admitted, or I must have spent the night in the street – there was nothing else for me; but, thank God! I've been spared that. On Christmas day I had a letter from my husband.

This she produced. It contained the following passage:

I am glad this letter only costs you a penny, as your purse must be getting very low; but there is a good time coming, and i trust in God it will not be long, my deir wife. i hope you will have got a good place before this raches you. I am dowing all in my power to help you. i trust in good in 3 months more, if you Help me, between us we make it out.

She concluded:

I wouldn't like him to know how badly I am off. He knows I would do nothing wrong. He wouldn't suspect me; he never would. He knows me too well. I have no clothes but what are detained for two shillings and sixpence, and what I have on. I have on just this shawl and an old cotton gown, but it's not broke, and my underclothing. All my wish is to get out to my husband. I care for nothing else in this world.[9]

A Girl Crossing-sweeper

I was told that a little girl formed one of the association of young sweepers, and at my request one of the boys went to fetch her.

She was a clean-washed little thing, with a pretty, expressive countenance, and each time she was asked a question she frowned, like a baby in its sleep, while thinking of the answer. In her ears she wore instead of rings loops of string, 'which the doctor had put there because her sight was wrong'. A cotton velvet bonnet, scarcely larger than the sun-shades worn at the sea-side, hung on her shoulders, leaving exposed her head, with the hair as rough as tow. Her green stuff gown was hanging in tatters, with long three-cornered rents as large as penny kites, showing the grey lining underneath; and her mantle was separated into so many pieces, that it was only held together by the braiding at the edge.

As she conversed with me, she played with the strings of her bonnet, rolling them up as if curling them, on her singularly small and also singularly dirty fingers.

I'll be fourteen, sir, a fortnight before next Christmas. I was born in Liquorpond Street, Gray's Inn Lane. Father come over from Ireland, and was a bricklayer. He had pains in his limbs and wasn't strong enough, so he give it over. He's dead now – been dead a longtime, sir. I was a littler girl then that I am now, for I wasn't above eleven at that time. I lived with mother after father died. She used to sell things in the streets – yes, sir, she was a coster. About a twelvemonth after father's death, mother was taken bad with the cholera, and died. I then went along with both grandmother and grandfather, who was a porter in Newgate Market; I stopped there until I got a place as servant of all-work. I was only turned, just turned, eleven then. I worked along with a French lady and gentleman in Hatton Garden, who used to give me a shilling a week and my tea. I used to go home to grandmother's to dinner every day. I hadn't to do any work, only just to clean the room and nurse the child. It was a nice little thing. I couldn't understand what the French people used to say, but there was a boy working there, and he used to explain to me what they meant.

I left them because they was going to a place called Italy – perhaps you may have heard tell of it, sir. Well, I suppose they must have been Italians, but we calls everybody, whose talk we don't understand, French. I went back to grandmother's, but, after grandfather died, she couldn't keep me, and so I went out begging – she sent me. I carried lucifer-matches and stay-laces first. I used to carry about a dozen laces, and perhaps I'd sell six out of them. I suppose I used to make about sixpence a day, and I used to take it home to grandmother, who kept and fed me.

At last, finding I didn't get much at begging, I thought I'd go crossing-sweeping. I saw other children doing it. I says to myself, 'I'll go and buy a broom', and I spoke to another little girl, who was sweeping up Holborn, who told me what I was to do. 'But,' says she, 'don't come and cut up me.'

I went first to Holborn, near to home, at the end of Red Lion Street. Then I was frightened of the cabs and carriages, but I'd get there early, about eight o'clock, and sweep the crossing clean, and I'd stand at the side on the pavement, and speak to the gentlemen and ladies before they crossed.

There was a couple of boys, sweepers at the same crossing before I went there. I went to them and asked if I might come and sweep there too, and they said Yes, if I would give them some of the halfpence I got. These was boys about as old as I was, and they said, if I earned sixpence, I was to give them twopence a-piece; but they never give me nothink of theirs. I never took more than sixpence, and out of that I had to give fourpence, so that I did not do so well as with the laces.

The crossings made my hands sore with the sweeping, and, as I got so little, I thought I'd try somewhere else. Then I got right down to the Fountings in Trafalgar Square, by the crossing at the statey on 'orseback. There were a good many boys and girls on that crossing at the time – five of them; so I went along with them. When I first went they said, 'Here's another fresh 'un.' They come up to me and says, 'Are you going to sweep here?' and I says, 'Yes'; and they says, 'You mustn't come here, there's too many'; and I says, 'They're different ones every day' – for they're not regular there, but shift about, sometimes one lot of boys and girls, and the next day another. They didn't say another word to me, and so I stopped.

It's a capital crossing, but there's so many of us, it spoils it. I seldom gets more than sevenpence a day, which I always takes home to grandmother.

I've been on that crossing about three months. They always calls me Ellen, my regular name, and behaves very well to me. If I see anybody coming, I call them out as the boys does, and then they are mine.

There's a boy and myself, and another strange girl, works on our side of the statey, and another lot of boys and girls on the other.

I like Saturdays the best day of the week, because that's the time as gentlemen as has been at work has their money, and then they are more generous. I gets more then, perhaps ninepence, but not quite a shilling, on the Saturday.

I've had a threepenny-bit give to me, but never sixpence. It was a gentleman, and I should know him again. Ladies gives me less than gentlemen. I foller 'em, saying, 'If you please, sir, give a poor girl a halfpenny'; but if the police are looking, I stop still.

I never goes out on Sunday, but stops at home with grandmother. I don't stop out at nights like the boys, but I gets home by ten at latest.[10]

An Irish Widower

One of these men had a half-shrewd, half-stolid look, and was clad in very dirty fustian. His beard was some days old, and he looked ill-fed and wretched. His children – for he had two boys with him, ten and twelve years old – were shoeless, their white skins being a contrast to their dirty dress, as the former appeared through the holes in their jackets. They looked on with a sort of vacant wonder, motionless, and without a word. The father said:–

I've been knocking about in England these four years from place to place. I'm telling you the truth, sir. [This he often repeated.] I came here to better myself, to knock out something better; but I wish to God I'd been buried before I buried my wife and children. I do, indeed, sir. I was a labourer in Ireland, working in farms and gardens for anybody. My wages warn't much, only three shillings a week, and my datal house [that is, a house rent-free], and two meals of victuals a day, sometimes 'taties and milk for meals, and sometimes 'taties and fish, and sometimes – aye, often – 'taties and nothing. My wife and me, and four children, came from Cork – it was in the county Cork I lived – to Wales. I don't know the name of the part; they've such queer names there; sure, then, they have, sir. It cost me half-a-crown a-piece for the six of us. I raised the money partly by digging up a garden I had, and selling what stuff there was, and the rest was made up by the farmers in the neighbourhood giving their threepence or sixpence a-piece to me, so that I might live. I wasn't on the poor-law rate, but I soon might. When I got to Wales, I had only sixpence left. I went to the workhouse for a night's lodging, to be sure – what else? I started next day for London with my wife and children, begging as we came, and going from workhouse to workhouse; and very badly we got along. It finished a fortnight to get to London. When we got to London (that's about four years agone) we got work at peas-picking, my wife and me, in the gardens about. That is for the summer. In the winter we sold oranges in the streets while she lived, and we had nothing from the parishes. I can't complain of the living till this time, sir; it was better than I knew in Ireland. I don't know what we got, she managed all. Last autumn we went into the hop county, to Ellis's farm. I don't know the town nearest; and there my wife and two children died of the cholera at the farm. The three of them weren't a week ill. The parish kept them and buried them. Since that I've been worse off than ever, and will always be worse off than ever, for I've lost a good wife. Since her death I jobbed about in the country, living very bare, me and the children, till the frost came, and then we came to London. I was knocking about for a fortnight, and begged a little; but sorrow a much I got by that. How did I know of this place? Musha, all the neighbours know about it.[11]

An Anxious Dog-collar Seller

He was sickly-looking, seemed dispirited at first, but to recover his spirits as he conversed, and spoke with a provincial (I presume a Warwickshire or Staffordshire) accent.

I served my time, sir; my relations put me – for my parents died when I was a boy – to a harness furniture maker, in [Walsall], who supplied Mr Dixon, a saddler's ironmonger, in a good way. I had fair makings, and was well treated, and when I was out of my time I worked for another master, and I then found I could make my pad territs [the round loops of the harness pad, through which the reins are passed], my hooks, my buckles, my ornaments (some of 'em crests), as well as any man. I worked only in brass, never plated, but sometimes the body for plating, and mostly territs and hooks. Thinking I'd better myself, I came to London. I was between five and six weeks before I got a stroke of work, and my money had gone. I found that London harness makers and coachmakers' names was put on Walsall-made goods, and 'London made' and 'town made' was put too. They might be as good, but they wasn't town made no more nor I am. I can't tell what I suffered, and felt, and thought, as at last I walked the streets. I was afraid to call at any brass-worker's – for I can do many sorts of brass work – I was so shabby. I called

once at Mr Arnold's, near Smithfield, and he, or his foreman perhaps it was, says to me, 'Give that tugbuckle a file.' I'd had nothing to eat but an apple I found in the street that day, and my hand trembled, and so he told me that drunkards, with trembling hands, wouldn't do there. I was never a drinking man; and at that time hadn't tasted so much as beer for ten days. My landlady – I paid her a shilling a week for half a bed with a porter – trusted me my rent, 'cause I paid her when I had it; but I walked about, nervous and trembling, and frightened at every sudden sound. I've stood looking over a bridge, but, though I may have thought of suicide, I never once had really a notion of it. I don't know how to tell it, but I felt stupefied like, as much as miserable. *I felt I could do nothing.* Perhaps I shouldn't have had power of mind to drown myself if I'd made up my resolution; besides, it's a dreadful wickedness. I always liked reading, and, before I was fairly beaten out, used to read at home, at shop-windows, and at bookstalls, as long as I dared, but latterly, when I was starving, I couldn't fix my mind to read anyhow.

One night I met a Walsall friend, and he took me to his inn, and gave me a good beef-steak supper and some beer, and he got me a nice clean bed in the house. In the morning he gave me what did me most good of all, a good new shirt, and five shillings. I got work two days after, and kept it near five years, with four masters, and married and saved £12. We had no family to live, and my poor wife died in the cholera in 1849, and I buried her decently, thank God, for she was a good soul. When I thought the cholera was gone, I had it myself, and was ill long, and lost my work, and had the same sufferings as before, and was without soles to my shoes or a shirt to my back, 'till a gentleman I'd worked for lent me a pound, and then I went into this trade, and pulled up a little. In six weeks I paid fifteen shillings of my debt, and had my own time for the remaining five shillings. Now I get an odd job with my master sometimes, and at others sell my collars, and chains, and key-rings, and locks, and such like. I'm ashamed of the dog-collar locks; I can buy them at two-pence a dozen, or one shilling and sixpence a gross; they're sad rubbish. In two or three weeks sometimes, the wire hasp is worn through, just by the rattling of the collar, and the lock falls off. I make now, one way and another, about ten shillings a week. My lodging's two shillings a week for a bedroom – it's a closet tho', for my furniture all went.

God's good, and I'll see better days yet. I have sure promise of regular work, and then I can earn thirty to forty shillings. I do best with my collars about the docks. I'm sure I don't know why.[12]

Flushermen

'It is a somewhat singular circumstance,' says Mr. Haywood, the City Surveyor, in his Report, dated February, 1850, 'that none of the men employed in the City sewers in flushing and cleansing, have been attacked with, or have died of, cholera during the past year; this was also the case in 1832–3. I do not state this to prove that the atmosphere of the sewers is not unhealthy – I by no means believe an impure atmosphere is healthy – but I state the naked fact, as it appears to me a some-what singular circumstance, and leave it to pathologists to argue upon.'

'I don't think flushing work disagrees with my husband,' said a flusherman's wife to me, 'for he eats about as much again at that work as he did at the other'.

'The smell underground is sometimes very bad,' said the man, 'but then we generally take a drop of rum first, and something to eat. It wouldn't do to go into it on an empty stomach, 'cause it would get into our inside. But in some sewers there's scarcely any smell at all. Most of the men are healthy who are engaged in it; and when the cholera was about many used to ask us how it was we escaped.'

The following statement contains the history of an individual flusherman:–

I was brought up to the sea, [he said] and served on board a man-of-war, the *Racer*, a 16-gun brig, laying off Cuba, in the West Indies, and thereaway, watching the slavers. I served seven years. We were paid off in '43 at Portsmouth, and a friend got me into the shores*. It was a great change from the open sea to a close shore – great; and I didn't like it at all at first. But it suits a married man, as I am now, with a family, much better than being a seaman, for a man aboard a ship can hardly do his children justice in their schooling and such like. Well, I didn't much admire going down the man-hole at first – the 'man-hole' is a sort of iron trap-door that you unlock and pull up; it leads to a lot of steps, and so you get into the shore – but one soon gets accustomed to anything. I've been at flushing and shore work now since '43, all but eleven weeks, which was before I got engaged.

We work in gangs from three to five men. I've been carried off my feet sometimes in the flush of a shore. Why, to-day, [a very rainy and windy day, Feb. 4] it came down Baker Street, when we flushed it, four foot plomb. It would have done for a mill-dam. One couldn't smoke or do anything. We can have a pipe and a chat now and then in the shore. The tobacco checks the smell. I can't say I felt the smell very bad when I first was in a shore. I've felt it worse since. I've been

* Sewers

made innocent drunk like in a shore by a drain from a distiller's. That happened me first in Vine Street shore, St Giles's, from Mr. Rickett's distillery. It came into the shore like steam. No, I can't say it tasted like gin when you breathed it – only intoxicating like. It was the same in Whitechapel from Smith's distillery. One night I was forced to leave off there, the steam had such an effect. I was falling on my back, when a mate caught me. The breweries have something of the same effect, but nothing like so strong as the distilleries. It comes into the shore from the brewers' places in steam. I've known such a steam followed by bushels of grains; ay, sir, cart-loads washed into the shore.

I never found anything in a shore worth picking up but once a half-crown. That was in the Buckingham Palace sewer. Another time I found sixteen shillings and sixpence, and thought that was a haul; but every bit of it, every coin, shillings and sixpences and joeys, was bad – all smashers. Yes, of course it was a disappointment, naturally so. That happened in Brick Lane shore, Whitechapel. O, somebody or other had got frightened, I suppose, and had shied the coins down into the drains. I found them just by the chapel there.

A second man gave me the following account of his experience in flushing:–

You remember, sir, that great storm on the 1st August, 1848. I was in three shores that fell in – Conduit Street and Foubert's Passage, Regent Street. There was then a risk of being drowned in the shores, but no lives were lost. All the house-drains were blocked about Carnaby Market – that's the Foubert's Passage shore – and the poor people was what you might call houseless. We got in up to the neck in water in some places, 'cause we had to stoop, and knocked about the rubbish as well as we could, to give a way to the water. The police put up barriers to prevent any carts or carriages going that way along the streets. No, there was no lives lost in the shores. One man was so overcome that he was falling off into a sort of sleep in Milford Lane shore, but was pulled out. I helped to pull him. He was as heavy as lead with one thing or other – wet, and all that. Another time, six or seven year ago, Whitechapel High Street shore was almost choked with butchers' offal, and we had a great deal of trouble with it.[13]

An Orphaned Street-girl

Father was a whitesmith [she said] and mother used to go out a-washing and a-cleaning, and me and my sister (but she is dead now) did nothing; we was sent to a day school, both of us. We lived very comfortable; we had two rooms and our own furniture; we didn't want for nothing when father was alive; he was very fond on us both, and was a kind man to everybody. He was took bad first when I was very young – it was consumption he had, and he was ill many years, about five years, I think it was, afore he died. When he was gone mother kept us both; she had plenty of work; she couldn't a-bear the thought of our going into the streets for a living, and we was both too young to get a place anywhere, so we stayed at home and went to school just as when father was alive. My sister died about two year and a half ago; she had the scarlet-fever dreadful, she lay ill seven weeks. We was both very fond of her, me and mother. I often wish she had been spared, I should not be alone in the world as I am now. We might have gone on together, but it is dreadful to be quite alone, and I often think now how well we could have done if she was alive.

Mother has been dead just a year this month; she took cold at the washing and it went to her chest; she was only bad a fortnight; she suffered great pain, and, poor thing, she used to fret dreadful, as she lay ill, about me, for she knew she was going to leave me. She used to plan how I was to do when she was gone. She made me promise to try to get a place and keep from the streets if I could, for she seemed to dread them so much. When she was gone I was left in the world without a friend. I am quite alone, I have no relation at all, not a soul belonging to me. For three months I went about looking for a place, as long as my money lasted, for mother told me to sell our furniture to keep me and get me clothes. I could have got a place, but nobody would have me without a character, and I knew nobody to give me one. I tried very hard to get one, indeed I did; for I thought of all mother had said to me about going into the streets. At last, when my money was just gone, I met a young woman in the street, and I asked her to tell me where I could get a lodging. She told me to come with her, she would show me a respectable lodging house for women and girls. I went, and I have been there ever since. The women in the house advised me to take to flower-selling, as I could get nothing else to do. One of the young women took me to market with her, and showed me how to bargain with the salesman for my flowers. At first, when I went out to sell, I felt so ashamed I could not ask anybody to buy of me; and many times went back at night with all my stock, without selling one bunch. The woman at the lodging-house is very good to me; and when I have a bad day she will let my lodging go until I can pay her. She always gives me my dinner, and a good dinner it is, of a Sunday; and she will often give me a breakfast, when she knows I have no money to buy any. She is very kind, indeed, for she knows I am alone. I feel very thankful to her, I am sure, for all her goodness to me. During the summer months I take one shilling and sixpence per day, which is sixpence profit. But I can only sell my flowers five days in the week – Mondays there is no flowers in the market – and of the sixpence a day I pay threepence for lodging. I get a halfpennyworth of tea; a halfpenny-worth of sugar; one pound of bread, a penny halfpenny; butter, a halfpenny. I never tastes meat but on Sunday. What I shall do in the winter I don't know. In the cold weather last year, when I could get no flowers, I was forced to live on my clothes, I have none left now but what I have on. What I shall do I don't know – I can't bear to think on it.[14]

A General Dealer

The general dealer 'works' everything through the season. He generally begins the year with sprats or plaice: then he deals in soles until the month of May. After this he takes to mackerel, haddocks, or red herrings. Next he trades in strawberries or raspberries. From these he will turn to green and ripe gooseberries; thence he will go to cherries; from cherries he will change to red or white currants; from them to plums or greengages, and from them again to apples and pears, and damsons. After these he mostly 'works' a few vegetables, and continues with them until the fish season begins again. Some general dealers occasionally trade in sweetmeats, but this is not usual, and is looked down upon by the 'trade'.

'I am a general dealer,' said one of the better class;

my missus is in the same line as myself, and sells everything that I do (barring green stuff). She follows me always in what I sell. She has a stall, and sits at the corner of the street. I have got three children. The eldest is ten, and goes out with me to call my goods for me. I have had inflammation in the lungs, and when I call my goods for a little while my voice leaves me. My missus is lame. She fell down a cellar, when a child, and injured her hip. Last October twelvemonth I was laid up with cold, which settled on my lungs, and laid me in my bed for a month. My missus kept me all that time. She was 'working' fresh herrings; and if it hadn't been for her we must all have gone into the workhouse. We are doing very badly now. I have no work to do. I have no stock-money to work with, and I object to pay one shilling and sixpence a week for the loan of ten shillings. Once I gave a man one and sixpence a week for ten months for the loan of ten shillings, and that nearly did me up. I have had eight shillings of the same party since, and paid a shilling a week for eight weeks for the loan of it. I consider it most extortionate to have to pay twopence a day for the loan of eight shillings, and won't do it. When the season gets a bit better I shall borrow a shilling of one friend and a shilling of another, and then muddle on with as much stock-money as I can scrape together.

My missus is at home now doing nothing. Last week it's impossible to say what she took, for we're obliged to buy victuals and firing with it as we take it. She can't go out charing on account of her hip. When she is out, and I am out, the children play about in the streets. Only last Saturday week she was obligated to take the shoes off her feet to get the children some victuals. We owe two week's rent, and the landlord, though I've lived in the house five years, is as sharp as if I was a stranger.[15]

Chapter Two: Disabled Bodies

The prevalence of birth defects was far greater in Victorian times than it is today. Poor maternal health led to congenital anomalies during the development of the foetus; there were also genetic anomalies, as a result of incest or cousin marriage. Of course, many of the severer defects led to early death, but those children who survived to adulthood, crippled or physically disabled in some other way, faced an even harder life than their able-bodied neighbours.

A Crippled Seller of Nutmeg-graters

I feel convinced that when the reader looks at the portrait here given, and observes how utterly helpless the poor fellow is, and then reads the following plain unvarnished tale, he will marvel like me, not only at the fortitude which could sustain him under all his heavy afflictions, but at the resignation (not to say philosophy) with which he bears them every one. His struggles to earn his own living (notwithstanding his physical incapacity even to put the victuals to his mouth after he has earned them) are instances of a nobility of pride that are I believe without a parallel. The poor creature's legs and arms are completely withered; indeed he is scarcely more than head and trunk. His thigh is hardly thicker than a child's wrist. His hands are bent inward from contraction of the sinews, the fingers being curled up and almost as thin as the claws of a bird's foot. He is unable even to stand, and cannot move from place to place but on his knees, which are shod with leather caps, like the heels of a clog, strapped round the joint; the soles of his boots are on the *upper* leathers, that being the part always turned towards the ground while he is crawling along. His countenance is rather handsome than otherwise; the intelligence indicated by his ample forehead is fully borne out by the testimony as to his sagacity in his business, and the mild expression of his eye by the statements as to his feeling for all others in affliction.

I sell nutmeg-graters and funnels [said the cripple to me]; I sell them at a penny and a penny halfpenny a piece. I get mine of the man in whose house I live. He is a tinman, and makes for the street trade and shops and all. I pay sevenpence a dozen for them, and I get a shilling or eighteenpence a dozen, if I can when I sell them, but I mostly get only a penny a piece – it's quite a chance if I have a customer at a penny halfpenny. Some days I sell only three – some days not one – though I'm out from ten o'clock till six. The most I ever took was three shillings and sixpence in a day. Some weeks I hardly clear my expenses – and they're between seven shillings and eight shillings a week; for not being able to dress and undress myself, I'm obligated to pay someone to do it for me – I think I don't clear more than seven shillings a week take one week with another. When I don't make that much, I go without – sometimes friends who are kind to me give me a trifle, or else I should starve. As near as I can judge, I *take* about fifteen shillings a week, and out of that I clear about six or seven shillings. I pay for my meals as I have them – threepence or fourpence a meal. I pay every night for my lodging as I go in, if I can; but if not my landlady lets it run a night or two. I give her a shilling a week for my washing and looking after me, and one and sixpence for my lodging. When I do very well I have three meals a day, but it's oftener only two – breakfast and supper – unless of Sunday. On a wet day when I can't get out, I often go without food. I may have a bit of bread and butter give me, but that's all – then I lie a-bed.

I feel miserable enough when I see the rain come down of a week day, I can tell you. Ah, it *is* very miserable indeed lying in bed all day, and in a lonely room, without perhaps a person to come near one – helpless as I am – and hear the rain beat against the windows, and all that without nothing to put in your lips. I've done *that* over and over again where I lived before; but where I am now I'm more comfortable like. My breakfast is mostly bread and butter and tea; and my supper, bread and butter and tea with a bit of fish, or a small bit of meat. What my landlord and landlady has I share with them. I never break my fast from the time I go out in the morning till I come home – unless it is a halfpenny orange I buy in the street; I do that when I feel faint. I have only been selling in the streets since this last winter. I was in the workhouse with a fever all the summer. I was destitute afterwards, and obliged to begin selling in the streets. The Guardians gave me five shillings to get stock. I had always dealt in tin ware, so I knew where to go to buy my things. It's very hard work indeed is street-selling for such as me. I can't walk no distance. I suffer a great deal of pains in my back and knees. Sometimes I go in a barrow, when I'm travelling any great way. When I go only a short way I crawl along on my knees and toes. The most I've ever crawled is two miles. When I get home afterwards, I'm in great pain. My knees swell dreadfully, and they're all covered with blisters, and my toes ache awful. I've corns all on top of them.

Often after I've been walking, my limbs and back ache so badly that I can get no sleep. Across my lines it feels as if I'd got some great weight, and my knees are in a heat, and throb, and feel as if a knife was running into them. When I go upstairs I have to crawl upon the back of my hands and my knees. I can't lift nothing to my mouth. The sinews of my hands is all contracted. I am obliged to have things held to my lips for me to drink, like a child. I *can* use a knife and fork by leaning my arm on the table and then stooping my head to it. I can't wash nor undress myself. Sometimes I think of my helplessness a great deal. The thoughts of it used to throw me into fits at one time – very bad. It's the Almighty's will that I am so, and I must abide by it. People says, as they passes me in the streets, 'Poor fellow, it's a shocking thing'; but very seldom they does any more than pity me; some lays out a halfpenny or a penny with me, but the most of 'em goes on about their business. Persons looks at me a good bit when I go into a strange place. I *do* feel it very much, that I haven't the power to get my living or to do a thing for myself, but I never begged for nothing. I'd sooner starve than I'd do that. I never thought that people whom God had given the power to help theirselves ought to help me. I *have* thought that I'm as I am, obliged to go on my hands and knees, from no fault of my own. Often I've done that, and I've over and over again laid in bed and wondered why the Almighty should send me into the world in such a state; often I've done that on a wet day, with nothing to eat, and no friend to come a-nigh me.

When I've gone along the streets, too, and been in pain, I've thought, as I've seen the people pass straight up, with all the use of their limbs, and some of them the biggest black-guards, cussing and swearing, I've thought, 'Why should I be deprived of the use of mine?' and I've felt angry like, and perhaps at that moment I couldn't bring my mind to believe the Almighty was so good and merciful as I'd heard say; but then in a minute or two afterwards I've prayed to Him to make me better and happier in the next world. I've always been led to think He's afflicted me as He has for some wise purpose or another that I can't see. I think as mine is so hard a life in this world, I shall be better off in the next. Often when I couldn't afford to pay a boy, I've not had my boots off for four or five nights and days, nor my clothes neither. Give me the world I couldn't take them off myself, and then my feet has swollen to that degree that I've been nearly mad with pain, and I've been shivering and faint, but still I was obliged to go out with my things; if I hadn't I should have starved. Such as I am can't afford to be ill – it's only rich folks as can lay up, not we; for us to take to our beds is to go without food altogether. When I was without never a boy, I used to tie the wet towel round the back of one of the chairs, and wash myself by rubbing my face up against it. I've been two days without a bit of anything passing between my lips. I couldn't go and beg for victuals – I'd rather go without. Then I used to feel faint, and my head used to ache dreadful. I used then to drink a plenty of water.

The women sex is mostly more kinder to me than the men. Some of the men fancies, as I goes along, that I can walk. They often says to me, 'Why, the sole of your boot is as muddy as mine'; and one on 'em is, because I always rests myself on that foot – the other sole, you see, is as clean as when it was first made. The women never seem frightened on me. My trade is to sell brooms and brushes, and all kinds of cutlery and tin-ware. I learnt it myself. I never was brought up to nothing, because I couldn't use my hands.

Mother was a cook in a nobleman's family when I were born. They say as I was a love-child. I was not brought up by mother, but by one of her fellow servants. Mother's intellects was so weak, that she couldn't have me with her. She used to fret a great deal about me, so her fellow servant took me when she got married. After I were born, mother married a farmer in middling circumstances. They tell me as my mother was frightened afore I was born. I never knew my father. He went over to Buonos Ayres, and kept an hotel there – I've heard mother say as much. No mother couldn't love a child more than mine did me, but her feelings was such she couldn't bear to see me. I never went to mother's to live, but was brought up by the fellow servant as I've told you of. Mother allowed her £30 a year. I was with her till two years back. She was always very kind to me – treated me like one of her own. Mother used to come and see me about once a year – sometimes not so often; she was very kind to me then. Oh, yes; I used to like to see her very much. Whatever I wished for she'd let me have; if I wrote to her, she always sent me what I wanted. I was very comfortably then.

Mother died four years ago; and when I lost her I fell into a fit – I was told of it all of a sudden. She and the party as I was brought up with was the only friends as I had in the world – the only persons as cared anything about a creature like me. I was in a fit for hours, and when I came to, I thought what would become of me: I knew I could do nothing for myself, and the only friend as I had as could keep me was gone. The person as brought me up was very good, and said, while she'd got a home I should never want; but, two years after mother's death, she was seized with the cholera, and then I hadn't a friend left in the world. When she died I felt ready to kill myself; I was all alone then, and what could I do, cripple as I was? She thought her sons and daughters as I'd been brought up with – like brothers and sisters – would look after me; but it was not in their power – they was only hard-working people. My mother used to allow so much a year for my schooling, and I can read and write pretty well. [He wrote his name in my presence kneeling at the table; holding the pen almost as one might fancy a bird would, and placing the paper sideways instead of straight before him.] While mother was alive, I was always foraging about to learn something unbeknown to her. I wanted to do so, in case mother should leave me without the means of getting a living. I used to buy old bedsteads, and take them to a man, and get him to repair them, and then I'd put the sacking on myself; I can hold a hammer somehow in my right hand. I used to polish them on my knees. I made a bench to my height out of two old chairs. I used to know what I should get for the bedsteads, and so could tell what I could afford to give the man to do up the parts as I couldn't manage. It was so I got to learn something like a business for myself. When the person died as had brought me up, I *could* do a little; I had then got the means. Before her death I had opened a kind of shop for things in the general line; I sold tin-ware, and brass-work, and candle-sticks, and fire-irons, and all old furniture, and gownprints as well.

I went into the tally business, and that ruined me alto-gether. I couldn't get my money in; there's a good deal owing to me now. Me and a boy used to manage the whole. I used to make all my account-books and everything. My lodgers didn't pay me my rent, so I had to move from the house, and live on what stock I had. In my new lodging I went on as well as I could for a little while; but about eighteen months ago I could hold on no longer. Then I borrowed a little, and went hawking tin-ware and brushes in the country. I sold baking-dishes, Dutch ovens, roastingjacks, skewers and gridirons, teapots, and saucepans, and combs. I used to exchange some-times for old clothes. I had a barrow and a boy with me; I used to keep him, and give him a shilling a week. I managed to get just a living that way. When the winter came on I gave it up; it was too cold. After that I was took bad with a fever; my stock had been all gone a little while before, and the boy had left because I couldn't keep him, and I had to do all for myself. All my friends was dead, and I had no one to help me, so I was obligated to lay about all night in my things, for I couldn't get them off alone; and that and want of food brought on a fever. Then I was took into the workhouse, and there I stopped all the summer, as I told you. I can't say they treated me bad, but they certainly didn't use me well. If I could have worked after I got better, I could have had tea; but 'cause I couldn't do nothing, they gave me that beastly gruel morning and night. I had meat three times a week. They would have kept me there till now, but I would die in the streets rather than be a pauper. So I told them, if they would give me the means of getting a stock, I would try and get a living for myself. After refusing many times to let me have ten shillings, they agreed to give me five shillings. Then I came out, but I had no home, and so I crawled about till I met with the people where I am now, and they let me sit up there till I got a room of my own. Then some of my friends collected for me about fifteen shillings altogether, and I did pretty well for a little while. I went to live close by the Blackfriars-road, but the people where I lodged treated me very bad. There was a number of girls of the town in the same street, but they was too fond of their selves and their drink to give nothing. They used to buy things of me and never pay me. They never made game of me, nor played me any tricks, and if they saw the boys doing it they would protect me. They never offered to give me no victuals; indeed, I shouldn't have liked to have eaten the food they got.

After that I couldn't pay my lodgings, and the parties where I lodged turned me out, and I had to crawl about the streets for four days and nights. This was only a month back. I was fit to die with pain all that time. If I could get a penny I used to go into a coffee-shop for half-a-pint of coffee, and sit there till they drove me out, and then I'd crawl about till it was time for me to go out selling. Oh! dreadful, dreadful, it was to be all them hours – day and night – on my knees. I couldn't get along at all, I was forced to sit down every minute, and then

I used to fall asleep with my things in my hand, and be woke up by the police to be pushed about and drove on by them. It seemed like as if I was walking on the bare bones of my knees. The pain in them was like the cramp, only much worse. At last I could bear it no longer, so I went afore Mr. Secker, the magistrate, at Union Hall, and told him I was destitute, and that the parties where I had been living kept my bed and the few things I had, for two shillings and sixpence rent, that I owed them. He said he couldn't believe that anybody would force me to crawl about the streets, for four days and nights, cripple as I was, for such a sum. One of the officers told him I was a honest and striving man, and the magistrate sent the officer, with the money, to get my things, but the landlady wouldn't give them till the officer compelled her, and then she chucked my bed out into the middle of the street. A neighbour took it in for me and took care of it till I found out the tinman who had before let me sit up in his house. I should have gone to him at first, but he lived farther than I could walk. I am stopping with him now, and he is very kind to me.

I have still some relations living, and they are well to do, but, being a cripple, they despise me. My aunt, my mother's sister, is married to a builder, in Petersham, near Richmond, and they are rich people – having some houses of their own besides a good business. I have got a boy to wheel me down on a barrow to them, and asked assistance of them, but they will have nothing to do with me. They won't look at me for my affliction. Six months ago they gave me half a crown. I had no lodgings nor victuals then; and *that* I shouldn't have had from them had I not said I was starving and must go to the parish. This winter I went to them, and they shut the door in my face. After leaving my aunt's, I went down to Ham Common, where my father-in-law lives, and there his daughter's husband sent for a policeman to drive me away from the place. I told the husband I had no money nor food; but he advised me to go begging, and said I shouldn't have a penny of them. My father-in-law was ill upstairs at the time, but I don't think he would have treated me a bit better – and all this they do because the Almighty has made me a cripple. I can, indeed, solemnly say, that there is nothing else against me, and that I strive hard and crawl about till my limbs ache enough to drive me mad, to get an honest livelihood. With a couple of pounds I could, I think, manage to shift very well for myself. I'd get a stock, and go into the country with a barrow, and buy old metal, and exchange tin ware for old clothes, and with that, I'm almost sure I could get a decent living. I'm accounted a very good dealer.

In answer to my inquiries concerning the character of this man, I received the following written communication:

I have known Charles Abbott twelve years; the last six years he has dealt with me for tinware. I have found him honest in all his dealings with me, sober and industrious.
Claud Hopman, Tinman.

From the writer of the above testimonial I received the following account of the poor cripple:

He is a man of generous a disposition, and very sensitive for the afflictions of others. One day while passing down the Borough he saw a man afflicted with St Vitus's dance shaking from head to foot, and leaning on the arm of a woman who appeared to be his wife.

The cripple told my informant that he should never forget what he felt when he beheld that poor man. '"I thought," he said, "what a blessing it is I am not like him."' Nor is the cripple, I am told, less independent than he is generous. In all his sufferings and privations he never pleads poverty to others; but bears up under the trials of life with the greatest patience and fortitude. When in better circumstances he was more independent than at present, having since, through illness and poverty, been much humbled.

'His privations have been great,' adds my informant. 'Only two months back, being in a state of utter destitution and quite worn out with fatigue, he called at the house of a person [where my informant occupied a room] about ten o'clock at night, and begged them to let him rest himself for a short while, but the inhuman landlady and her son laid hold of the wretched man, the one taking him by the arms and the other by the legs, and literally hurled him into the street. The next morning,' my informant continued, 'I saw the poor creature leaning against a lamp-post, shivering with the cold, and my heart bled for him; and since that he has been living with me.'[16]

A Crossing-sweeper with a Wooden Leg

This man lives up a little court running out of a wide, second-rate street. It is a small court, consisting of some half-dozen houses, all of them what are called by courtesy 'private'.

I inquired at No. 3 for John Simmons; 'The first-floor back, if you please, sir'; and to the first-floor back I went.

Here I was answered by a good-looking and intelligent young woman, with a baby, who said her husband had not yet come home, but would I walk in and wait? I did so; and found myself in a very small, close room, with a little furniture, which the man called 'his few sticks', and presently discovered another child – a little girl. The girl was very shy in her manner, being only two years and two months old, and as her mother said, very ailing from the difficulty of cutting her teeth, though the true cause seemed to be want of proper nourishment and fresh air. The baby was a boy – a fine, cheerful, good-tempered little fellow, but rather pale, and with an unnaturally large forehead. The mantel-piece of the room was filled with little ornaments of various sorts, such as bead-baskets, and over them hung a series of black profiles – not portraits of either the crossing-sweeper or any of his family, but an odd lot of heads, which had lost their owners many a year, and served, in company with a little red, green, and yellow scripture-piece, to keep the wall from looking bare. Over the door (inside the room) was nailed a horse-shoe, which, the wife told me, had been put there by her husband, for luck.

A bed, two deal tables, a couple of boxes, and three chairs, formed the entire furniture of the room, and nearly filled it. On the window frame was hung a small shaving-glass; and on the two boxes stood a wicker-work apology for a perambulator, in which I learnt the poor crippled man took out his only daughter at half-past four in the morning. 'If some people was to see that, sir,' said the sweeper, when he entered and saw me looking at it, 'they would, and in fact they *do* say, "Why, you can't be in want." Ah! little they know how we starved and pinched our-selves before we could get it.'

There was a fire in the room, notwithstanding the day was very hot; but the window was wide open, and the place tolerably ventilated, though oppressive. I have been in many poor people's 'places', but never remember one so poor in its appointments and yet so free from effluvia.

The crossing-sweeper himself was a very civil sort of man, and in answer to my inquiries said:

I know that I do as I ought to, and so I don't feel hurt at standing at my crossing. I have been there four years. I found the place vacant. My wife, though she looks very well, will never be able to do any hard work; so we sold our mangle, and I took to the crossing: but we're not in debt, and nobody can't say nothing to us. I like to go along the streets free of such remarks as is made by people to whom you owes money. I had a mangle in Bell's Yard, but through my wife's weakness I was forced to part with it. I was on the crossing a short time before that, for I knew that if I parted with my mangle and things before I knew whether I could get a living at the crossing I couldn't get my mangle back again.

We sold the mangle only for a sovereign, and we gave two pounds ten shillings for it; we sold it to the same man that we bought it of. About six months ago I managed for to screw and save enough to buy that little wicker chaise, for I can't carry the children because of my one leg, and of course the mother can't carry them both out together. There was a man had the crossing I've got; he died three or four years before I took it; but he didn't depend on the crossing – he did things for the tradespeople about, such as carpet-beating, messages, and so on.

When I first took the crossing I did very well. It happened to be a very nasty, dirty season, and I took a good deal of money. Sweepers are not always civil, sir.

I wish I had gone to one of the squares, though. But I think after Farringdon Street is paved with stone I shall do better. I am certain I never taste a bit of meat from one week's end to the other. The best day I ever made was five and sixpence or six shillings; it was the winter before last. If you remember, the snow laid very thick on the ground, and the sudden thaw made walking so uncomfortable, that I did very well. I have taken as little as sixpence, fourpence, and even twopence. Last Thursday I took two ha'pence all day. Take one week with the other, seven or eight shillings is the very outside.

I don't know how it is, but some people who used to give me a penny don't now. The boys who come in wet weather earn a great deal more than I do. I once lost a good chance, sir, at the corner of the street leading to Cavendish-square. There's a bank, and they pay a man seven shillings a week to sweep the crossing: a butcher in Oxford Market spoke for me; but when I went up, it unfortunately turned out that I was not fit, from the loss of my leg. The last man they had there they were obliged to turn away – he was so given to drink.

I think there are some rich crossing sweepers in the city, about the Exchange; but you won't find them now during this dry weather, except in by-places. In wet weather, there are two or three boys who sweep near my crossing, and take all my earnings away. There's a great able-bodied man besides – a fellow strong enough to follow the plough. I said to the policeman, 'Now, ain't this a shame?' and the policeman said, 'Well, *he* must get his living as well as you.' I'm always civil to the police, and they're always civil to me – in fact, I think sometimes I'm too civil – I'm not rough enough with people.

You soon tell whether to have any hopes of people coming across. I can tell a gentleman directly I see him. Where I stand, sir, I could get people in trouble everlasting; there's all sorts of thieving going on. I saw the other day two or three respectable persons take a purse out of an old lady's pocket before the baker's shop at the corner; but I can't say a word, or they would come and throw me into the road. If a gentleman gives me sixpence, he don't give me any more for three weeks or a month; but I don't think I've more than three or four gentlemen as gives me that. Well, you can scarcely tell the gentleman from the clerk, the clerks are such great swells now.

Lawyers themselves dress very plain; those great men who don't come every day, because they've clerks to do their business for them, they give most. People hardly ever stop to speak unless it is to ask you where places are – you might be occupied at that all day. I manage to pay my rent out of what I take on Sunday, but not lately – this weather religious people go pleasuring. I'd like to go to church, if I could, but when I come home I am tired; but I've got books here, and they do as well, sir. I read a little and write a little.

I lost my leg through a swelling – there was no chloroform then. I was in the hospital three years and a half, and was about fifteen or sixteen when I had it off. I always feel the sensation of the foot, and more so at change of weather. I feel my toes moving about, and everything; sometimes, it's just as if the calf of my leg was itching. I *feel* the rain coming; when I see a cloud coming my leg shoots, and I know we shall have rain.

My mother was a laundress – my father has been dead nineteen years my last birthday. My mother was subject to fits, so I was forced to stop at home to take care of the business.

I am at my crossing at half-past eight; at half-past eleven I come home to dinner. I go back at one or two till seven.

Sometimes I mind horses and carts, but the boys get all that business. One of these little customers got sixpence the other day for only opening the door of a cab. I don't know how it is they let these little boys be about; if I was the police, I wouldn't allow it.

I think it's a blessing, having children [referring to his little girl] – that child wants the gravy of meat, or an egg beaten up, but she can't get it. I take her out every morning round Euston Square and those open places. I get out about half-past four. It is early, but if it benefits her, that's no odds.[17]

A Peep-show Exhibitor

Being a cripple, I am obliged to exhibit a small peep-show. I lost the use of this arm ever since I was three months old. My mother died when I was ten years old, and after that my father took up with an Irishwoman, and turned me and my youngest sister (she was two years younger than me) out into the streets. My father had originally been a dyer, but was working at the fiddlestring business then. My youngest sister got employment at my father's trade, but I couldn't get no work, because of my crippled arms. I walked about till I fell down in the streets for want. At last a man, who had a sweetmeat shop, took pity on me. His wife made the sweetmeats, and minded the shop while he went out a-juggling in the streets, in the Ramo Samee line. He told me as how, if I would go round the country with him, and sell prints while he was a-juggling in the public-houses, he'd find me in vittles and pay my lodging. I joined him, and stopped with him two or three year.

After that, I went to work for a very large waste-paper dealer. He used to buy up all the old back numbers of the cheap periodicals and penny publications, and send me out with them to sell at a farthing a-piece. He used to give me fourpence out of every shilling, and I done very well with that, till the periodicals came so low, and so many on 'em, that they wouldn't sell at all. Sometimes I could make fifteen shillings on a Saturday night and a Sunday morning, aselling the odd numbers of periodicals, such as 'Tales of the Wars', 'Lives of the Pirates', 'Lives of the Highwaymen' &c. I've often sold as many as 2,000 numbers on a Saturday night in the New Cut, and the most of them was works about thieves, and highwaymen, and pirates. Besides me there was three others at the same business. Altogether, I dare say, my master alone used to get rid of 10,000 copies of such works on a Saturday night and Sunday morning. Our principal customers was young men. My master made a good bit of money at it. He had been about eighteen years in the business, and had begun with two shillings and sixpence. I was with him fifteen year on and off, and at the best time I used to earn my thirty shillings a week full at that time. But then I was foolish, and didn't take care of my money.

When I was at the 'odd-number business' I bought a peep-show. I gave two pounds ten shillings for it. I had it second-hand. I was persuaded to buy it. A person as has got only one hand, you see, isn't like other folks, and the people said it would always bring me a meal of victuals, and keep me from starving. The peep-shows was a-doing very well then (that's about five or six years back), when the theatres was all a shilling to go into them whole price, but now there's many at threepence and twopence, and a good lot at a penny. Before the theatres lowered, a peep-showman could make three or four shillings a day, at the least, in fine weather, and on a Saturday night about double that money. At a fair he could take his fifteen shillings to a pound a day. Then there was about nine or ten peep-shows in London.

These were all back-shows. There are two kinds of peep-shows, which we call 'back-shows' and 'caravan-shows'. The caravan-shows are much larger than the others, and are drawn by a horse or a donkey. They have a green-baize curtain at the back, which shuts out them as don't pay. The showmen usually lives in these caravans with their families. Often there will be a man, his wife, and three or four children, living in one of these shows. These caravans mostly go into the country, and very seldom are seen in town. They exhibit principally at fairs and feasts, or wakes, in country villages. They generally go out of London between March and April, because some fairs begin at that time, but many wait for the fairs at May. Then they work their way right round, from village to town. They tell one another what part they're agoing to, and they never interfere with one another's rounds. If a new hand comes into the business, they're very civil, and tells him what places to work. The caravans comes to London about October, after the fairs is over.

The scenes of them caravan shows is mostly upon recent battles and murders. Anything in that way, of late occurrence, suits them. Theatrical plays ain't no good for country towns, 'cause they don't understand such things there. People is very fond of the battles in the country, but a murder wot is well known is worth more than all the fights. There was more took with Rush's murder than there has been even by the Battle of Waterloo itself. Some of the caravan-shows does very well. Their average taking is thirty shillings a week for the summer months. At some fairs they'll take £5 in the three days. They have been about town as long as we can recollect. I should say there is full fifteen of these caravan shows throughout the country. Some never comes into London at all. There is about a dozen that comes to London regular every winter. The business in general goes from family to family. The cost of a caravan-show, second-hand, is £40; that's without the glasses, and them runs from ten shillings to a pound apiece, because they're large. Why, I've knowed the front of a peep-show, with the glasses, cost £60; the front was mahogany, and had thirty-six glasses, with gilt carved mouldings round each on 'em. The scenes will cost about £6 if done by the best artist, and £3 if done by a common hand.

The back-shows are peepshows that stand upon trussels, and are so small as to admit of being carried on the back. The scenery is about 18 inches to 2 foot in length, and about 15 inches high. They have been introduced about fifteen or sixteen years. The man as first brought 'em up was named Billy Tomkins; he was lame of one leg, and used to exhibit little automaton figures in the New Cut. On their first coming out, the oldest back-showman as I know on told me they could take fifteen shillings a day. But now we can't do more than seven shillings a week, run Saturday and all the other days together, – and that's through the theatres being so low. It's a regular starving life now. We has to put up with the insults of people so. The back-shows generally exhibits plays of different kinds what's been performed at the theatres lately. I've got many different plays to my show. I only exhibit one at a time. There's 'Halonzer the Brave and the Fair Himogen'; 'The Dog of Montargis and the Forest of Bondy'; 'Hyder Halley, or the Lions of Mysore'; 'The Forty Thieves' (that never done no good to me); 'The Devil and Dr Faustus'; and at Christmas time we exhibit pantomimes. I has some other scenes as well. I've 'Napoleon's Return from Helba'; 'Napoleon at Waterloo'; 'The Death of Lord Nelson'; and also 'The Queen embarking to start for Scotland, from the Dockyard at Woolwich'. We takes more from children than grown people in London, and more from grown people than children in the country. You see, grown people has such re-marks made upon them when they're apeeping through in London, as to make it bad for us here. Lately I have been hardly able to get a living, you may say. Some days I've taken sixpence, others eightpence and sometimes a shilling – that's what I call a good day for any of the week-days. On a Saturday it runs from two shillings to two shillings and sixpence. Of the week-days, Monday or Tuesday is the best. If there's a fair on near London, such as Greenwich, we can go and take three shillings, and four shillings, or five shillings a day, so long as it lasts. But after that, we comes back to the old business, and that's bad enough; for, after you've paid one shilling and sixpence a week rent, and sixpence a week stand for your peep-show, and come to buy a bit of coal, why all one can get is a bit of bread and a cup of tea to live upon. As for meat, we don't see it from one month's end to the other. My old woman, when she is at work, only gets five fardens a-pair for making a pair of drawers to send out for the convicts, and three halfpence for a shirt; and out of that she has to find her own thread.[18]

An Afflicted Crossing-sweeper

Passing the dreary portico of the Queen's Theatre, and turning to the right down Tottenham Mews, we came upon a flight of steps leading up to what is called 'The Gallery', where an old man, gasping from the effects of a lung disease, and feebly polishing some old harness, proclaimed himself the father of the sweeper I was in search of, and ushered me into the room where he lay a-bed, having had a 'very bad night'.

The room itself was large and of a low pitch, stretching over some stables; it was very old and creaky (the sweeper called it 'an old wilderness') and contained, in addition to two turn-up bedsteads, that curious medley of articles which, in the course of years, an old and poor couple always manage to gather up. There was a large lithograph of a horse, dear to the remembrance of the old man from an indication of a dog in the corner. 'The very spit of the one I had for years; it's a real portrait, sir, for Mr. Hanbart, the printer, met me one day and sketched him.' There was an etching of Hogarth in a black frame; a stuffed bird in a wooden case, with a glass before it; a piece of painted glass, hanging in a place of honour, but for which no name could be remembered, excepting that it was 'of the old-fashioned sort'. There were the odd remnants, too, of old china ornaments, but very little furniture; and, finally, a kitten.

The father, worn out and consumptive, had been groom to Lord Combermere. 'I was with him, sir, when he took Bonyparte's house at Malmasong. I could have had a pension then if I'd a liked, but I was young and foolish, and had plenty of money, and we never know what we may come to.'

The sweeper, although a middle-aged man, had all the appearance of a boy – his raw-looking eyes, which he was always wiping with a piece of linen rag, gave him a forbidding expression, which his shapeless, short, bridgeless nose tended to increase. But his manners and habits were as simple in their character as those of a child; and he spoke of his father's being angry with him for not getting up before, as if he were a little boy talking of his nurse.

He walks, with great difficulty, by the help of a crutch; and the sight of his weak eyes, his withered limb, and his broken shoulder (his old helpless mother, and his gasping, almost inaudible father) form a most painful subject for compassion.

The crossing-sweeper gave me, with no little meekness and some slight intelligence, the following statement:

I very seldom go out on a crossin' o' Sundays. I didn't do much good at it. I used to go to church of a Sunday – in fact, I do now when I'm well enough.

It's fifteen year next January since I left Regent Street. I was there three years, and then I went on Sundays occasionally. Sometimes I used to get a shilling, but I have given it up now – it didn't answer; besides, a lady who was kind to me found me out, and said she wouldn't do any more for me if I went out on Sundays. She's been dead these three or four years now.

When I was at Regent Street I might have made twelve shillings a week, or something thereabout.

I am seven-and-thirty the twenty-sixth day of last month, and I have been lame six-and-twenty years. My eyes have been bad ever since my birth. The scrofulous disease it was that lamed me – it come with a swelling on the knee, and the outside wound broke about the size of a crown piece, and a piece of bone come from it; then it gathered in the inside and at the top. I didn't go into the hospital then, but I was an outpatient, for the doctor said a close confined place wouldn't do me no good. He said that the seaside would, though; but my parents couldn't afford to send me, and that's how it is. I *did* go to Brighton and Margate nine years after my leg was bad, but it was too late then.

I have been in Middlesex Hospital, with a broken collarbone, when I was knocked down by a cab. I was in a fortnight there, and I was in again when I hurt my leg. I was sweeping my crossin' when the top came off my crutch. I fell back'ards, and my leg doubled under me. They had to carry me there.

I went into the Middlesex Hospital for my eyes and leg. I was in a month, but they wouldn't keep me long, there's no cure for me.

My leg is very painful, 'specially at change of weather. Sometimes I don't get an hour's sleep of a night – it was daylight this morning before I closed my eyes.

I went on the crossing first because my parents couldn't keep me, not being able to keep theirselves. I thought it was the best thing I could do, but it's like all other things, it's got very bad now. I used to manage to rub along at first – the streets have got shockin' bad of late.

To tell the truth, I was turned away from Regent Street by Mr. Cook, the furrier, corner of Argyle Street. I'll tell you as far as I was told. He called me into his passage one night, and said I must look out for another crossin', for a lady, who was a very good customer of his, refused to come while I was there; my heavy afflictions was such that she didn't like the look of me. I said, 'Very well'; but because I come there next day and the day after that, he got the policeman to turn me away. Certainly the policeman acted very kindly, but he said the gentleman wanted me removed, and I must find another crossing.

Then I went down Charlotte Street, opposite Percy Chapel, at the corner of Windmill Street. After that I went to Wells Street, by getting permission of the doctor at the corner. He thought that it would be better for me than Charlotte Street, so he let me come. Ah! there ain't so many crossing-sweepers as there was; I think they've done away with a great many of them.

When I first went to Wells Street, I did pretty well, because there was a dress-maker's at the corner, and I used to get a good deal from the carriages that stopped before the door. I used to take five or six shillings in a day then, and I don't take so much in a week now. I tell you what I made this week. I've made one and fourpence, but it's been so wet, and people are out of town; but, of course, it's not always alike – sometimes I get three and sixpence or four shillings. Some people gives me a sixpence or a fourpenny-bit; I reckons that all in.

I am dreadful tired when I comes home of a night. Thank God my other leg's all right! I wish the t'other was as strong, but it never will be now.

The police never try to turn me away; they're very friendly, they'll pass the time of day with me, or that, from knowing me so long in Oxford Street.

My broom sometimes serves me a month; of course, they don't last long now it's showery weather. I give twopence-halfpenny a piece for 'em, or threepence.

I don't know who gives me the most; my eyes are so bad I can't see. I think, though, upon an average, the gentlemen give most. Often I hear the children, as they are going by, ask their mothers for something to give to me; but they only say, 'Come along – come along!' It's very rare that they lets the children have a ha'penny to give me.

My mother is seventy the week before next Christmas. She can't do much now; she does though go out on Wednesdays or Saturdays, but that's to people she's known for years who is attached to her. She does her work there just as she likes. Sometimes she gets a little washing – sometimes not. This week she had a little, and was forced to dry it indoors; but that makes 'em half dirty again. My father's breath is so bad that he can't do anything except little odd jobs for people down here; but they've got the knack now, a good many on 'em, of doin' their own.

We have lived here fifteen years next September; it's a long time to live in such an old wilderness, but my old mother is a sort of woman as don't like movin' about, and I don't like it. Some people are everlasting on the move. When I'm not on my crossin' I sit poking at home, or make a job of mending my clothes. I mended these trousers in two or three places.

It's all done by feel, sir. My mother says it's a good thing we've got our feeling at least, if we haven't got our eyesight.[19]

A Writer Without Hands

A man of sixty-one, born in the crippled state he described, tall, and with an intelligent look and good manners, gave me this account:

I was born without hands – merely the elbow of the right arm and the joint of the wrist of the left. I have rounded stumps. I was born without feet also, merely the ankle and heel, just as if my feet were cut off close within the instep. My father was a farmer in Cavan County, Ireland, and gave me a fair education. He had me taught to write. I'll show you how, sir.

Here he put on a pair of spectacles, using his stumps, and then holding the pen on one stump, by means of the other he moved the two together, and so wrote his name in an old-fashioned hand.

I was taught by an ordinary schoolmaster. I served an apprenticeship of seven years to a turner, near Cavan, and could work well at the turning, but couldn't chop the wood very well. I handled my tools as I've shown you I do my pen. I came to London in 1814, having a prospect of getting a situation in the India house; but I didn't get it, and waited for eighteen months, until my funds and my father's help were exhausted, and I then took to making fancy screens, flower-vases, and hand-racks in the streets. I did very well at them, making fifteen shillings to £1 a week in the summer, and not half that, perhaps not much more than a third, in the winter. I continue this work still, when my health permits, and I now make handsome ornaments, flower-vases, etc. for the quality, and have to work before them frequently, to satisfy them. I could do very well but for ill-health. I charge from five shillings to eight shillings for hand-screens, and from seven and sixpence to fifteen shillings for flower-vases. Some of the quality pay me handsomely – some are very near. I have done little work in the streets this way, except in very fine weather. Sometimes I write tickets in the street at a halfpenny each. The police never interfere unless the thoroughfare is obstructed badly. My most frequent writing is, 'Naked came I into the world, and naked shall I return.' 'The Lord giveth, and the Lord taketh away; blessed be the name of the Lord.' To that I add my name, the date sometimes, and a memorandum that it was the writing of a man born without hands or feet.

When I'm not disturbed, I do pretty well, getting one and sixpence a day; but that's an extra day. The boys are a great worry to me. Working people are my only friends at the writing, and women the best. My best pitches are Tottenham Court Road and the West End thoroughfares. There's three men I know who write without hands. They're in the country chiefly, travelling. One man writes with his toes, but chiefly in the public-houses, or with showmen. I consider that I am the only man in the world who is a handicraftsman without hands or feet.

I am married, and have a grown-up family. Two of my sons are in America, one in Australia, one a sailor, the others are emigrants on the coast of Africa, and one a cabinet-maker in London – all fine fellows, well made. I had fifteen in all. My father and mother, too, were a handsome, wellmade couple.[20]

Chapter Three: Dangerous Work

The health of working people in dangerous jobs was largely left in their own hands. There were few regulations governing working conditions. If someone had an accident as a result of his job, there were plenty more people eager for the work. Even the amount of work a man was expected to do was uncontrolled, and anyone who failed to meet excessive targets could be shoved aside.

An Overworked Man

Never in all my experience had I seen so sad an instance of overwork. The poor fellow was so fatigued that he could hardly rest in his seat. As he spoke he sighed deeply and heavily, and appeared almost spirit-broken with excessive labour:

I work at what is called a strapping shop, and have worked at nothing else for these many years past in London. I call 'strapping' doing as much work as a human being or a horse possibly can in a day, and that without any hanging upon the collar, but with the foreman's eyes constantly fixed upon you, from six o'clock in the morning to six o'clock at night. The shop in which I work is for all the world like a prison; the silent system is as strictly carried out there as in a model gaol. If a man was to ask any common question of his neighbour, except it was connected with his trade, he would be discharged there and then. If a journeyman makes the least mistake, he is packed off just the same. A man working at such places is almost always in fear; for the most trifling things he's thrown out of work in an instant. And then the quantity of work that one is forced to get through is positively awful; if he can't do a plenty of it, he don't stop long where I am. No one would think it was possible to get so much out of blood and bones. No slaves work like we do. At some of the strapping shops the foreman keeps continually walking about with his eyes on all the men at once. At others the foreman is perched high up, so that he can have the whole of the men under his eye together. I suppose since I knew the trade that a *man does four times the work that he did formerly.* I know a man that's done four pairs of sashes in a day, and one is considered to be a good day's labour.

What's worse than all, the men are every one striving one against the other. Each is trying to get through the work quicker than his neighbours. Four or five men are set the same job, so that they may be all pitted against one another, and then away they go every one striving his hardest for fear that the others should get finished first. They are all tearing along from the first thing in the morning to the last at night, as hard as they can go, and when the time comes to knock off they are ready to drop. I was hours after I got home last night before I could get a wink of sleep; the soles of my feet were on fire, and my arms ached to that degree that I could hardly lift my hand to my head. Often, too, when we get up of a morning, we are more tired than when we went to bed, for we can't sleep many a night; but we mustn't let our employers know it, or else they'd be certain we couldn't do enough for them, and we'd get the sack. So, tired as we may be, we are obliged to look lively, somehow or other, at the shop of a morning. If we're not beside our bench the very moment the bell's done ringing, our time's docked – they won't give us a single minute out of the hour. If I was working for a fair master, I should do nearly one-third, and sometimes a half, less work than I am now forced to get through, and, even to manage that much, I shouldn't be idle a second of my time.

It's quite a mystery to me how they *do* contrive to get so much work out of the men. But they are very clever people. They know how to have the most out of a man, better than anyone in the world. They are all picked men in the shop – regular 'strappers' and no mistake. The most of them are five foot ten, and fine broad-shouldered, strong-backed fellows too – if they weren't they wouldn't have them. Bless you, they make no words with the men, they sack them if they're not strong enough to do all they want; and they can pretty soon tell, the very first shaving a man strikes in the shop, what a chap is made of. Some men are done up at such work – quite old men and gray with spectacles on, by the time they are forty. I have seen fine strong men, of thirty-six, come in there and be bent double in two or three years. They are most all countrymen at the strapping shops. If they see a great strapping fellow, who they think has got some stuff about him that will come out, they will give him a job directly.

We are used for all the world like cab or omnibus horses. Directly they've had all the work out of us, we are turned off, and I am sure, after my day's work is over, my feelings must be very much the same as one of the London cab horses. As for Sunday, it is literally a day of rest with us, for the greater part of us lay a-bed all day, and even that will hardly take the aches and pains out of our bones and muscles. When I'm done and flung by, of course I must starve.[21]

A Maimed Irish Crossing-sweeper

He stands at the corner of Brewer Street, where the yellow omnibuses stop, and refers to himself every now and then as the 'poor lame man'. He has no especial mode of addressing the passers-by, except that of hobbling a step or two towards them and sweeping away an imaginary accumulation of mud. He has lost one leg (from the knee) by a fall from a scaffold, while working as a bricklayer's labourer in Wales, some six years ago; and speaks bitterly of the hard time he had of it when he first came to London, and hobbled about selling matches. He says he is thirty-six, but looks more than fifty; and his face has the ghastly expression of death. He wears the ordinary close cloth street-cap and corduroy trousers. Even during the warm weather he wears an upper coat – a rough thick garment, fit for the Arctic regions. It was very difficult to make him understand my object in getting information from him: he thought that he had nothing to tell, and laid great stress upon the fact of his never keeping 'count' of anything.

He accounted for his miserably small income by stating that he was an invalid – 'now and thin continually'. He said:

I can't say how long I have been on this crossin'; I think about five year. When I came on it there had been no one here before. No one interferes with me at all, at all. I never hard of a crossin' bein' sold; but I don't know any other sweepers. I makes no freedom with no one, and I always keeps my own mind.

I dunno how much I earn a day – p'rhaps I may get a shilling, and p'rhaps sixpence. I didn't get much yesterday [Sunday] – only sixpence. I was not out on Saturday; I was ill in bed, and I was at home on Friday. Indeed, I did not get much on Thursday, only tuppence ha'penny. The largest day? I dunno. Why, about a shilling. Well, sure, I might get as much as two shillings, if I got a shillin' from a lady. Some gentlemen are good – such a gentleman as you, now, might give me a shilling.

Well, as to weather, I likes half dry and half wet; of course I wish for the bad weather. Every one must be glad of what brings good to him; and, there's one thing, I can't make the weather – I can't make a fine day nor a wet one. I don't think anybody would interfere with me; certainly, if I was a blaggard I should not be left here; no, nor if I was a thief; but if any other man was to come on to my crossing, I can't say whether the police *would* interfere to protect me – p'rhaps they might.

What is it I say to shabby people? Well, by Jesus, they're all shabby, I think. I don't see any difference; but what can I do? I can't insult them, and I was never insulted myself, since here I've been, nor, for the matter of that, ever had an angry word spoken to me.

Well, sure, I dunno who's the most liberal; if I got a four-penny bit from a moll I'd take it. Some of the ladies are very liberal; a good lady will give a sixpence. I never hard of sweepin' the mud back again; and as for the boys annoying me, I has no coleaguein' with boys, and they wouldn't be allowed to interfere with me – the police wouldn't allow it.

After I came from Wales, where I was on one leg, selling matches, then it was I took to sweep the crossin'. A poor devil must put up with anything, good or bad. Well, I was a labourin' man, a bricklayer's labourer, and I've been away from Ireland these sixteen year. When I came from Ireland I went to Wales. I was there a long time; and the way I broke my leg was, I fell off a scaffold. I am not married; a lame man wouldn't get any woman to have him in London at all, at all. I don't know what age I am. I am not fifty, nor forty; I think about thirty-six. No, by Jesus, it's not myself that ever knew a well-off crossin' sweeper. I don't deal in them at all.

I got a deal of friends in London assist me (but only now and then). If I depended on the few ha'pence I get, I wouldn't live on 'em; what money I get here wouldn't buy a pound of mate; and I wouldn't live, only for my friends. You see, sir, I can't be out always. I am laid up nows and thens continually. Oh, it's a poor trade to big on the crossin' from morning till night, and not get sixpence. I couldn't do with it, I know.

Yes, sir, I smoke; it's a comfort, it is. I like any kind I'd get to smoke. I'd like the best if I got it.

I am a Roman Catholic, and I go to St Patrick's, in St Giles's; a many people from my neighbourhood go there. I go every Sunday, and to confession just once a-year – that saves me.

By the Lord's mercy! I don't get broken victuals, nor broken mate, not as much as you might put on the tip of a fork; they'd chuck it out in the dust-bin before they'd give it to me. I suppose they're all alike.

The devil an odd job I ever got, master, nor knives to clean. If I got their knives to clean, p'rhaps I might clean them.

My brooms cost threepence ha'penny; they are very good. I wear them down to a stump, and they last three weeks, this fine wither. I never got any old clothes – not but I want a coat very bad, sir.

I come from Dublin; my father and mother died there of cholera; and when they died, I come to England, and that was the cause of my coming.

By my oath it didn't stand me in more than eighteenpence that I took here last week. I live in Crook Lane, St Giles's Church, on the second landing, and I pay eightpence a week. I haven't a room to myself, for there's a family lives in it with me.

When I goes home I just smokes a pipe, and goes to bed, that's all.[22]

Chimney Sweeps

The house was rented by a sweeper, a master on his own account, and every room in the place was let to sweepers and their wives or women, which, with these men, often signify one and the same thing. The inside of the house looked as dark as a coalpit; there was an insufferable smell of soot, always offensive to those unaccustomed to it; and every person and every thing which met the eye, even to the caps and gowns of the women, seemed as if they had just been steeped in Indian ink.

In one room was a sweep and his woman quarrelling. As I opened the door I caught the words, 'I'm damned if I has it any longer. I'd see you bloody well damned first, and you knows it.' The savage was intoxicated, for his red eyes flashed through his sooty mask with drunken excitement, and his matted hair, which looked as if it had never known a comb, stood out from his head like the whalebone ribs of his own machine. 'Bloody Bet', as he called her, did not seem a whit more sober than her man; and the shrill treble of her voice was distinctly audible till I turned the corner of the street, whither I was accompanied by the master of the house, to whom I had been recommended by one of the fraternity as an intelligent man, and one who knew 'a thing or two'.

'You see,' he said, as we turned the corner, 'there isn't no use a talkin' to them 'ere fellows – they're all tosticated now, and they doesn't care nothink for nobody; but they'll be quiet enough tomorrow, 'cept they yarns somethink, and if they do then they'll be just as bad to-morrow night. They're a awful lot, and nobody will never do anythink with them.

From him I obtained the following statement:

I was a climbing-boy, and served a regular apprenticeship for seven years. I was out on my apprenticeship when I was fourteen. Father was a silk-weaver, and did all he knew to keep me from being a sweep, but I would be a sweep, and nothink else. [This is not so very uncommon a predilection, strange as it may seem.] So father, when he saw it was no use, got me bound apprentice. Father's alive now, and near ninety years of age. I don't know why I wished to be a sweep, 'cept it was this – there was sweeps always lived about here, and I used to see the boys with lots of money a tossin' and gamblin', and wished to have money too. You see they got money where they swept the chimneys; they used to get twopence or threepence for theirselves in a day, and sometimes sixpence from the people of the house, and that's the way they always had plenty of money.

I never thought anythink of the climbing; it wasn't so bad as some people would make you believe. There are two or three ways of climbing. In wide flues you climb with your elbows and your legs spread out, your feet pressing against the sides of the flue; but in narrow flues, such as nine-inch ones, you must slant it; you must have your sides in the angles, it's wider there, and go up just that way. [Here he threw himself into position – placing one arm close to his side, with the palm of the hand turned outwards, as if pressing the side of the flue, and extending the other arm high above his head, the hand apparently pressing in the same manner.] There, that's slantin'. You just put yourself in that way, and see how small you make yourself.

I never got to say stuck myself, but a many of them did; yes, and were taken out dead. They were smothered for want of air, and the fright, and a stayin' so long in the flue; you see the waistband of their trousers sometimes got turned down in the climbing, and in narrow flues, when not able to get it up, then they stuck. I had a boy once – we were called to sweep a chimney down at Poplar. When we went in he looked up the flues. 'Well, what is it like?' I said. 'Very narrow,' says he, 'don't think I can get up there'; so after some time we gets on top of the house, and takes off the chimney pot, and has a look down – it was wider a' top, and I thought as how he could go down. 'You had better buff it, Jim,' says I. I suppose you know what that means; but Jim wouldn't do it, and kept his trousers on. So down he goes, and gets on very well till he comes to the shoulder of the flue, and then he couldn't stir. He shouts down, 'I'm stuck.' I shouts up and tells him what to do. 'Can't move,' says he, 'I'm stuck hard and fast.'

Well, the people of the house got fretted like, but I says to them, 'Now my boy's stuck, but for Heaven's sake don't make a word of noise; don't say a word, good or bad, and I'll see what I can do.' So I locks the door, and buffs it, and forces myself up till I could reach him with my hand, and as soon as he got his foot on my hand he begins to prise himself up, and gets loosened, and comes out at the top again. I was stuck myself, but I was stronger nor he, and I manages to get out again. Now I'll be bound to say if there was another master there as would kick up a row and a-worried, that ere boy 'ud a never come out o' that 'ere flue alive. There was a many o' them lost their lives in that way.

Most all the apprentices used to come from the 'House' [workhouse]. There was nobody to care for them, and some masters used them very bad. I was out of my time at fourteen, and began to get too stout to go up the flues; so after knockin' about for a year or so, as I could do nothink else, I goes to sea on board a man-of-war, and was away four year. Many of the boys, when they got too big and useless, used to go to sea in them days – they couldn't do nothink else. Yes, many of them went for soldiers; and I know some who went for Gipsies, and others who went for play-actors, and a many who got on to be swellmobsmen, and thieves, and housebreakers, and the like o' that ere. There ain't nothink o' that sort a-goin' on now since the Ack of Parliament.

When I got back from sea father asked me to learn his business; so I takes to the silk-weaving and learned it, and then married a weaveress, and worked with father for a long time. Father was very well off – well off and comfortable for a poor man – but trade was good then. But it got bad afterwards, and none on us was able to live at it; so I takes to the chimney-sweeping again. A man might manage to live somehow at the sweeping, but the weaving was o' no use. It was the foreign silks as beat us all up, that's the whole truth. Yet they tells us as how they was a-doin' the country good; but they may tell that to the marines – the sailors won't believe it – not a word on it. I've stuck to the sweeping ever since, and sometimes done very fair at it; but since the Ack there's so many leeks come to it that I don't know how they live – they must be eatin' one another up.[23]

A Bearded Crossing-sweeper

Since the destruction by fire of the Royal Exchange in 1838, there has been added to the curiosities of Cornhill a thickset, sturdy, and hirsute crossing-sweeper – a man who is as civil by habit as he is independent by nature. He has a long flowing beard, grey as wood smoke, and a pair of fierce moustaches, giving a patriarchal air of importance to a marked and observant face, which often serves as a painter's model. After half-an-hour's conversation, you are forced to admit that his looks do not all belie him, and that the old mariner (for such was his profession formerly) is worthy in some measure of his beard.

He wears an old felt hat – very battered and discoloured – around his neck, which is bared in accordance with sailor custom; he has a thick blue cotton neckerchief tied in a sailor's knot; his long iron-grey beard is accompanied by a healthy and almost ruddy face. He stands against the post all day, saying nothing, and taking what he can get without solicitation.

When I first spoke to him, he wanted to know to what purpose I intended applying the information that he was prepared to afford, and it was not until I agreed to walk with him as far as St Mary Axe that I was enabled to obtain his statement, as follows:

I've had this crossing ever since '38. The Exchange was burnt down in that year. Why, sir, I was wandering about trying to get a crust, and it was very sloppy, so I took and got a broom; and while I kept a clean crossing, I used to get ha'pence and pence. I got a dockman's wages – that's half-a-crown a day; sometimes only a shilling, and sometimes more. I have taken a crown – but that's very rare. The best customers I had is dead. I used to make a good Christmas, but I don't now. I have taken a pound or thirty shillings then in the old times.

I smoke, sir; I will have tobacco, if I can't get grub. My old woman takes cares that I have tobacco.

I have been a sailor, and the first ship as ever I was in was the old *Colossus*, 74, but we was only cruising about the Channel then, and took two prizes. I went aboard the old *Remewa* guardship – we were turned over to her – and from her I was drafted over to the *Escramander* frigate. We went out chasing Boney, but he gived himself up to the old *Impregnable*. I was at the taking of Algiers, in 1816, in the *Superb*. I was in the *Rochfort*, 74, up the Mediterranean (they call it up the Mediterranean, but it was the Malta station) three years, ten months, and twenty days, until the ship was paid off.

Then I went to work at the dockyard. I had a misfortune soon after that. I fell out of a garret window, three stories high, and that kept me from going to the docks again. I lost all my top teeth by that fall. I've got a scar here, one on my chin; but I warn't in the hospital more than two weeks.

I was afeard of being taken up solicitin' charity, and I knew that sweeping was a safe game; they couldn't take me up for sweeping a crossing.

Sometimes I get insulted, only in words; sometimes I get chaffed by sober people. Drunken men I don't care for; I never listen to 'em, unless they handle me, and then, although I am sixty-three this very day, sir, I think I could show them something. I do carry my age well; and if you could ha' seen how I have lived this last winter through, sometimes one pound of bread between two of us, you'd say I was a strong man to be as I am.

Those who think that sweepin' a crossing is idle work make a great mistake. In wet weather, the traffic that makes it gets sloppy as soon as it's cleaned. Cabs, and 'busses, and carriages continually going over the crossing must scatter the mud on it, and you must look precious sharp to keep it clean; but when I once get in the road, I never jump out of it. I keeps my eye both ways, and if I gets in too close quarters, I slips round the wheels. I've had them almost touch me.

No, sir, I never got knocked down. In foggy weather, of course, it's no use sweeping at all.

Parcels! It's very few parcels I get to carry now; I don't think I get a parcel to carry once in a month: there's 'busses and railways so cheap. A man would charge as much for a distance as a cab would take them.

I don't come to the same crossing on Sundays; I go to the corner of Finch Lane. As to regular customers, I've none – to say regular; some give me sixpence now and then. All those who used to give me regular are dead.

I was a-bed when the Exchange was burnt down.

I have had this beard five years. I grew it to sit to artists when I got the chance; but it don't pay expenses – for I have to walk four or five miles, and only get a shilling an hour: besides, I'm often kept nearly two hours, and I get nothing for going and nothing for coming, but just for the time I am there.

Afore I wore it, I had a pair of large whiskers. I went to a gentleman then, an artist, and he did pay me well. He advised me to grow mustarshers and the beard, but he hasn't employed me since.

They call me 'Old Jack' on the crossing, that's all they call me. I get more chaff from the boys than any one else. They only say, 'Why don't you get shaved?' but I take no notice on 'em.

Old Bill, in Lombard Street! I knows him; he used to make a good thing of it, but I don't think he makes much now.

My wife – I am married, sir – doesn't do anything. I live in a lodging-house, and I pay three shillings a week. I tell you what we has, now, when I go home. We has a pound of bread, a quarter of an ounce of tea, and perhaps a red herring.

I've had a weakness in my legs for two year; the veins comes down, but I keep a bandage in my pocket, and when I feels 'em coming down, I puts the bandage on 'till the veins goes up again – it's through being on my legs so long (because I had very strong legs when young) and want of good food. When you only have a bit of bread and a cup of tea – no meat, no vegetables – you find it out; but I'm as upright as a dart, and as lissome as ever I was.

I gives threepence for my brooms. I wears out three in a week in the wet weather. I always lean very hard on my broom, 'specially when the mud is sticky – as it is after the roads is watered. I am very particular about my brooms; I gives 'em away to be burned when many another would use them.[24]

A Hot-eel Man

'I was a coalheaver,' he said to me, as I sat in his attic up a close court, watching his wife 'thicken the liquor';

I was a-going along the plank, from one barge to another, when the swell of some steamers throwed the plank off the 'horse', and chucked me down, and broke my knee against the side of the barge. Before that I was yarning upon an average my twenty to thirty shillings a week. I was seven months and four days in King's College Hospital after this. I found they was a-doing me no good there, so I come out and went over to Bartholemy's Hospital. I was in there nineteen months altogether, and after that I was a month in Middlesex Hospital, and all on 'em turned me out incurable. You see, the bone's decayed – four bits of bone have been taken from it. The doctor turned me out three times 'cause I wouldn't have it off. He asked my wife if she would give consent, but neither she nor my daughter would listen to it, so I was turned out on 'em all.

How my family lived all this time it's hard to tell. My eldest boy did a little – got three shillings and sixpence a week as an errand-boy, and my daughter was in service, and did a little for me; but that was all we had to live upon. There was six children on my hands, and however they *did* manage I can't say. After I came out of the hospital I applied to the parish, and was allowed two shillings and sixpence a week and four loaves. But I was anxious to do something, so a master butcher, as I knowed, said he would get me 'a pitch' [the right to fix a stall], if I thought I could sit at a stall and sell a few things. I told him I thought I could, and would be very thankful for it. Well, I had heard how the man up in the market was making a fortune at the hot-eel and pea-soup line. [A paviour as left his barrow and two shovels with me told me to-day, said the man, by way of parenthesis – 'that he knowed for a fact he was clearing £6 a week regular'.] So I thought I'd have a touch at the same thing. But you see, I never could rise money enough to get sufficient stock to make a do of it, and never shall, I expect – it don't seem like it, however. I ought to have five shillings to go to market with tomorrow, and I ain't got above one and sixpence; and what's that for stockmoney, I'd like to know? Well, as I was saying, the master butcher lent me ten shillings to start in the line. He was the best friend I ever had. But I've never been able to do anything at it – not to say to get a living.

'He can't carry anything now, sir,' said his wife, as the old man strove to get the bellows to warm up the large kettle of pea-soup that was on the fire.

Aye, I can't go without my crutch. My daughter goes to Billingsgate for me. I've got nobody else; and she cuts up the eels. If it warn't for her I must give it up altogether, and go into the workhouse outright. I couldn't fetch 'em. I ought to have been out tonight by rights till ten, if I'd had anything to have sold. My wife can't do much; she's troubled with the rheumatics in her head and limbs.

'Yes,' said the old body, with a sigh, 'I'm never well, and never shall be again, I know.'

'Would you accept on a drop of soup, sir?' asked the man. 'You're very welcome, I can assure you. You'll find it very good, sir.' I told him I had just dined, and the poor old fellow proceeded with his tale.

Last week I earned clear about eight shillings, and that's to keep six on us. I didn't pay no rent last week nor yet this, and I don't know when I shall again, if things goes on in this way. The week before there was a fast-day, and I didn't earn above six shillings that week, if I did that. My boy can't go to school. He's got no shoes nor nothing to go in. The girls go to the ragged-school, but we can't send them of a Sunday nowhere.

'Other people can go,' said one of the young girls nestling round the fire, and with a piece of sacking over her shoulders for a shawl – 'them as has got things to go in; but mother don't like to let us go as we are'.

She slips her mother's shoes on when she goes out. It would take a pound to start me well. With that I could go to market, and buy my draught of eels a shilling cheaper, and I could afford to cut my pieces a little bigger; and people where they gets used well comes again – don't you see? I could have sold more eels if I'd had 'em to-day, and soup too. Why, there's four hours of about the best time tonight that I'm losing now 'cause I've nothing to sell. The man in the market can give more than we can. He gives what is called the lumping ha'p'orth – that is, seven or eight pieces; ah, that I daresay he does; indeed, some of the boys has told me he gives as many as eight pieces. And then the more eels you boils up, you see, the richer the liquor is, and in our little tin-pot way it's like boiling up a great joint of meat in a ocean of water. In course we can't compete against the man in the market, and so we're being ruined entirely. The boys very often comes and asks me if I've got a farden's-worth of heads. The woman at Broadway, they tells me, sells 'em at four a farden and a drop of liquor, but we chucks 'em away, there's nothing to eat on them; the boys though will eat anything.[25]

A Disabled Coalwhipper

Hearing that accidents were frequent among [the coalwhippers], I was anxious to see a person who had suffered by the danger of the calling. A man was brought to me with his hand bound up in a handkerchief. The sleeve of his coat was ripped open and dangled down beside his injured arm. He walked lame; and on my inquiring whether his leg was hurt, he began pulling up his trousers and unlacing his boot, to show me that it had not been properly set. He had evidently once been a strong, muscular man, but little now remained as evidence of his physical power but the size of his bones. He furnished me with the following statement:

I was a coalwhipper. I had a wife and two children. Four months ago, coming off my day's work, my foot slipped, and I fell and broke my leg. I was taken to the hospital, and remained there ten weeks. At the time of my accident I had no money at all by me, but was in debt to the amount of ten shillings to my landlord. I had a little furniture, and a few clothes of myself and wife. While I was in the hospital, I did not receive anything from our benefit society, because I had not been able to keep up my subscription. My wife and children lived while I was in the hospital by pawning my things, and going from door to door to everyone she knowed to give her a bit. The men who worked in the same gang as myself, made up four shillings and sixpence for me, and that, with two loaves of bread that they had from the relieving officer, was all they got.

While I was in the hospital the landlord seized for rent the few things that my wife had not pawned, and turned her and my two little children into the street. One was a boy three years old, and the other a baby just turned ten months.

My wife went to her mother, and she kept her and my little ones for three weeks, till she could do so no longer. My mother, poor old woman, was 'most as bad off as we were. My mother only works on the ground, out in the country, at gardening. She makes about seven shillings a week in the summer, and in the winter she has only ninepence a day to live upon; but she had at least a shelter for her child, and she willingly shared that with her daughter and her daughter's children. She pawned all the clothes she had, to keep them from starving; but at last everything was gone from the poor old woman, and then I got my brother to take my family in. My brother worked at garden-work, the same as my mother-in-law did. He made about fifteen shillings a week in the summer, and about half that in the winter time. He had a wife and two children of his own, and found it hard enough to keep them, as times go. But still he took us all in, and shared what he had with us, rather than let us go to the workhouse. When I was told to leave the hospital – which I was forced to do upon my crutches, for my leg was very bad still – my brother took me in too. He had only one room, but he got in a bundle of straw for me, and we lived and slept there for seven weeks. He got credit for more than a pound's worth of bread, and tea, and sugar for us; and now he can't pay, and the man threatens to summon him for it.

After I left my brother's, I came to live in the neighbourhood of Wapping, for I thought I might manage to do a day's work at coalwhipping, and I couldn't bear to live upon his little earnings any longer – he could scarcely keep himself then. At last I got a ship to deliver; but I was too weak to do the work, and in pulling at the ropes my hands got sore, and festered for want of nourishment. [He took the handkerchief off and showed that it was covered with plaster. It was almost white from deficient circulation.] After this I was obliged to lay up again, and that's the only job of work I've been able to do for these last four months. My wife can't do anything; she is a delicate, sickly little woman as well, and has the two little children to mind, and to look after me likewise. I had one pennyworth of bread this morning. We altogether had half-a-quartern loaf among the four of us, but no tea nor coffee. Yesterday we had some bread, and tea, and butter; but wherever my wife got it from I don't know. I was three days but a short time back without a taste of food. [Here he burst out crying.] I had nothing but water that passed my lips. I had merely a little at home, and that my wife and children had. I would rather starve myself than let them do so: indeed, I've done it over and over again. I never begged: I'll die in the streets first. I never told nobody of my life. The foreman of my gang was the only one besides God that knew of my misery; and his wife came to me and brought me money and brought me food, and himself, too, many a time.

'I had a wife and five children of my own to maintain, and it grieved me to my heart,' said the man who sat by, 'to see them want, and I unable to do more for them'.

'If any accident occurs to any of us who are not upon the society,' the coalwhipper continued, 'they must be as bad off as I am. If I only had a little nourishment to strengthen me, I could do my work again; but, poor as I am, I can't get strength to do it, and not being totally incapacitated from ever resuming my labour, I cannot get any assistance from the superannuation fund of our men.'

I told the man I wished to see him at his own home, and he and the foreman who had brought him to me, and who gave him a most excellent character, led me into a small house in a court near the Shadwell entrance to the London Docks. When I reached the place I found the room almost bare of furniture.

A baby lay sprawling on its back on a few rags beside the handful of fire. A little shoeless boy, with only a light washed-out frock to cover him, ran shyly into a corner of the room as we entered. There was only one chair in the room, and that had been borrowed from downstairs. Over the chimney hung to dry a few ragged infant's chemises that had been newly washed. In front of the fire, on a stool, sat the thinly-clad wife; and in the corner of the apartment stood a few old tubs. On a line above these were two tattered men's shirts, hanging to dry, and a bed was thrown on some boxes. On a shelf stood a physic-bottle that the man had got from the parish doctor, and in the empty cupboard was a slice of bread – all the food, they said, they had in the world, and they knew not where on earth to look for more.[26]

A Coal-backer

I've worked at backing since I was twenty-four, and that's more than twelve years ago. I limit myself now, because times is not so good, to two pots of beer a day; that is, when I'm all day at work. Some takes more. I reckon, that when times was better I drank fifteen pots a week, for I was in regular work, and middlin' well off. That's 780 pots, or 195 gallons a year, you say. Like enough it may be. I never calculated, but it does seem a deal. It can't be done without, and men themselves is the best judges of what suits their work – I mean, of how much to take. I'll tell you what it is, sir. Our work's harder than people guess at, and one must rest sometimes. Now, if you sit down to rest without something to refresh you, the rest does you harm instead of good, for your joints seem to stiffen; but a good pull at a pot of beer backs up the rest, and we start lightsomer. Our work's very hard. I've worked till my head's ached like to split; and when I've got to bed, I've felt as if I've had the weight on my back still, and I've started awake when I fell off to sleep, feeling as if something was crushing my back flat to my chest. I can't say that I ever tried to do without beer altogether. If I was to think of such a thing, my old woman there would think I was out of my head. [The wife assented.]

I've often done with a little when work's been slackish. First, you see, we bring the coal up from the ship's hold. There, sometimes, it's dreadful hot, not a mouthful of air, and the coal-dust sometimes as thick as a fog. You breathe it into you, and your throat's like a flue, so that you must have something to drink. I fancy nothing quenches you like beer. We want a drink that tastes. Then there's the coals on your back to be carried up a nasty ladder, or some such contrivance, perhaps twenty feet, and a sack full of coals weighs two hundredweight and a stone, at least; the sack itself's heavy and thick: isn't that a strain on a man? No horse could stand it long. Then, when you get fairly out of the ship, you go along planks to the waggon, and must look sharp, 'specially in slippery or wet weather, or you'll topple over, and then there's the hospital or the workhouse for you. Last week we carried along planks sixty feet, at least. There's nothing extra allowed for distance, but there ought to be.

I've sweat to that degree in summer, that I've been tempted to jump into the Thames to cool myself. The sweat's run into my boots, and I've felt it running down me for hours as I had to trudge along. It makes men bleed at the nose and mouth, this work does. Sometimes we put a bit of coal in our mouths, to prevent our biting our tongues. I do, sometimes, but it's almost as bad as if you did bite your tongue, for when the strain comes heavier and heavier on you, you keep scrunching the coal to bits, and swallow some of it, and you're half choked; and then it's no use, you must have beer. Some's tried a bit of tobacco in their mouths, but that doesn't answer; it makes you spit, and often spit blood. I know I can't do without beer. I don't think they 'dulterate it for us; they may for fine people, that just tastes it, and, I've heard, has wine and things. But we must have it good, and a publican knows who's good customers. Perhaps a bit of good grub might be as good as beer to strengthen you at work, but the straining and sweating makes you thirsty, more than hungry; and if poor men must work so hard, and for so little, for rich men, why poor men will take what they feel will satisfy them, and run the risk of its doing them good or harm; and that's just where it is. I can't work three days running now without feeling it dreadful. I get a mate that's fresher to finish my work. I'd rather earn less at a trade that would give a man a chance of some ease, but all trades is overstocked. You see we have a niceish tidy room here, and a few middling sticks, so I can't be a drunkard.[27]

The Mother of a Featherhouse Worker

When I saw the mother, she carried a great-coat, as she was on her way to the stall; and she used it as ladies do their muffs, burying her hands in it. The mother's dark-coloured old clothes seemed, to borrow a description from Sir Walter Scott, flung on with a pitchfork. These two women were at first very suspicious, and could not be made to understand my object in questioning them; but after a little while, the mother became not only communicative, but garrulous, conversing – with no small impatience at any interruption – of the doings of the people in her neighbourhood. I was accompanied by an intelligent costermonger, who assured me of his certitude that the old woman's statement was perfectly correct, and I found moreover from other inquiries that it was so.

'Well, sir,' she began, 'what is it that you want of me? Do I owe you anything? There's half-pay officers about here for no good; what is it you want? Hold your tongue, you young fool [to her daughter, who was beginning to speak], 'what do you know about it?' [On my satisfying her that I had no desire to injure her, she continued, to say after spitting, a common practice with her class, on a piece of money, 'for luck']:

Certainly, sir, that's very proper and good. Aye, I've seen the world – the town world and the country. I don't know where I was born; never mind about that – it's nothing to nobody. I don't know nothing about my father and mother; but I know that afore I was eleven I went through the country with my missis. She was a smuggler. I didn't know then what smuggling was – bless you, sir, I didn't; I knew no more nor I know who made that lamp-post. I didn't know the taste of the stuff we smuggled for two years – didn't know it from small beer; I've known it well enough since, God knows. My missis made a deal of money that time at Deptford Dockyard. The men wasn't paid and let out till twelve of a night – I hardly mind what night it was, days was so alike then – and they was our customers till one, two, or three in the morning – Sunday morning, for anything I know. I don't know what my missis gained; something jolly, there's not a fear of it. She was kind enough to me.

I don't know how long I was with missis. After that I was a hopping, and made my fifteen shillings regular at it, and at haymaking; but I've had a pitch at my corner for thirty-eight year – aye! turned thirty-eight. It's no use asking me what I made at first – I can't tell; but I'm sure I made more than twice as much as my daughter and me makes now, the two of us. I wish people that thinks we're idle now were with me for a day. I'd teach them. I don't – that's the two of us don't – make fifteen shillings a week now, nor the half of it, when all's paid. Damned if I do. The damned boys take care of that. [Here I had a statement of the boy's tradings, similar to what I have given.]

There's 'Canterbury' has lots of boys, and they bother me. I can tell, and always could, how it is with working men. When mechanics is in good work, their children has halfpennies to spend with me. If they're hard up, there's no halfpennies. The pennies go to a loaf or to buy a candle. I might have saved money once, but had a misfortunate family. My husband? O, never mind about him. Damn him. I've been a widow many years. My son – it's nothing how many children I have – is married; he had the care of an engine. But he lost it from ill health. It was in a featherhouse, and the flue got down his throat, and coughed him; and so he went into the country, 108 miles off, to his wife's mother. But his wife's mother got her living by wooding, and other ways, and couldn't help him or his wife; so he left, and he's with me now. He has a job sometimes with a greengrocer, at sixpence a day and a bit of grub; a little bit – very. I must shelter him. I couldn't turn him out. If a Turk I knew was in distress, and I had only half a loaf, I'd give him half of that, if he was ever such a Turk – I would, sir! Out of sixpence a day, my son – poor fellow, he's only twenty-seven! – wants a bit of 'baccy and a pint of beer. It 'ud be unnatural to oppose that, wouldn't it, sir? He frets about his wife, that's staying with her mother, 108 miles off; and about his little girl; but I tell him to wait, and he may have more little girls. God knows, they come when they're not wanted a bit.

I joke and say all my old sweethearts is dying away. Old Jemmy went off sudden. He lent me money sometimes, but

I always paid him. He had a public once, and had some money when he died. I saw him the day afore he died. He was in bed, but wasn't his own man quite; though he spoke sensible enough to me. He said, said he, 'Won't you have half a quartern of rum, as we've often had it?' 'Certainly, Jemmy,' says I, 'I came for that very thing.' Poor fellow! His friends are quarrelling now about what he left. It's £56 they say, and they'll go to law very likely, and lose every thing. There'll be no such quarrelling when I die, unless it is for the pawn-tickets. I get a meal now, and got a meal afore; but it was a better meal then, sir. Then look at my expenses. I was a customer once. I used to buy, and plenty such did, blue cloth aprons, opposite Drury Lane theatre: the very shop's there still, but I don't know what it is now; I can't call to mind. I gave two shillings and sixpence a yard, from twenty to thirty years ago, for an apron, and it took two yards, and I paid fourpence for making it, and so an apron cost five shillings and fourpence –that wasn't much thought of in those times. I used to be different off then.

I never go to church; I used to go when I was a little child at Sevenoaks. I suppose I was born somewhere thereabouts. I've forgot what the inside of a church is like. There's no costermongers ever go to church, except the rogues of them, that wants to appear good. I buy my fruit at Covent Garden. Apples is now four shillings and sixpence a bushel there. I may make twice that in selling them; but a bushel may last me two, three, or four days.[28]

Chapter Four: Losing Sight

Among the working people Mayhew met in the streets of London, there were a large number of people who were blind, either from birth or as a result of an infection or injury later in life. For many of them, their blindness was just one of the many difficulties facing poor working people in London, and in a remarkable series of interviews, Mayhew uncovered a surprising acceptance of their lot, with some people rising above their disability to remain cheerful and get on with daily life.

A Blind Silhouette-cutter

A cheerful blind man, well known to all crossing Waterloo or Hungerford Bridges, gave me the following account of his figurecutting:

I had the measles when I was seven, and became blind; but my sight was restored by Dr Jeffrey, at old St George's Hospital. After that I had several relapses into total blindness in consequence of colds, and since 1840 I have been quite blind, excepting that I can partially distinguish the sun and the gas-lights, and such-like, with the left eye only. I am now thirty-one, and was brought up to house-painting. When I was last attacked with blindness I was obliged to go into St Martin's workhouse, where I underwent thirteen operations in two years. When I came out of the workhouse I played the German flute in the street, but it was only a noise, not music, sir. Then I sold boot-laces and tapes in the street, and averaged five shillings a week by it – certainly not more. Next I made little wooden tobacco stoppers in the street, in the shape of legs – they're called 'legs'. The first day I started in that line – it was in Tottenham Court Road – I was quite elated, for I made half-a-crown. I next tried it by St Clement's Church, but I found that I cut my hands so with the knives and files, that I had to give it up, and I then took up with the trade of cutting out profiles of animals and birds, and grotesque human figures, in card. I established myself soon after I began this trade by the Victoria-gate, Bayswater; that was the best pitch I ever had – one day I took fifteen shillings, and I averaged thirty shillings a week for six weeks. At last the inspector of police ordered me off. After that I was shoved about by the police, such crowds gathered round me, until I at length got leave to carry on my business by Waterloo Bridge; that's seven years ago. I remained there till the opening of Hungerford Bridge, in May 1845.

I sit there cold or fine, winter or summer, every day but Sunday, or if I'm ill. I often hear odd remarks from people crossing the bridge. In winter time, when I've been cold and hungry, and so poor that I couldn't get my clothes properly mended, one has said, 'Look at that poor blind man there'; and another (and oft enough, too) has answered, 'Poor blind man! He has better clothes and more money than you or me; it's all done to excite pity!' I can generally tell a gentleman's or lady's voice, if they're the real thing. I can tell a purseproud man's voice, too. He says, in a domineering, hectoring way, as an ancient Roman might speak to his slave, 'Ah, ha! My good fellow! How do you sell these things?' Since January last, I may have averaged eight shillings a week – that's the outside. The working and the middling classes are my best friends. I know of no other man in my particular line, and I've often inquired concerning any.[29]

A Blind Street-reader

An intelligent man gave me the following account of his experience as a blind reader. He was poorly dressed, but clean, and had not a vulgar look:

My father died when I was ten years old, and my mother in the coronation year, 1838. I am now in my thirty-eighth year. I was a clerk in various offices. I was not born blind, but lost my sight four years ago, in consequence of aneurysm. I was a fortnight in the Ophthalmic Hospital, and was an out-patient for three months. I am a married man, with one child, and we did as well as we could, but that was very badly, until every bit of furniture (and I had a house full of good furniture up to that time) went.

At last I thought I might earn a little by reading in the street. The Society for the Indigent Blind gave me the Gospel of St John, after Mr. Freer's system, the price being eight shillings; and a brother-in-law supplied me with the Gospel of St Luke, which cost nine shillings. In Mr. Freer's system the regular alphabet letters are not used, but there are raised characters, thirty-four in number, including long and short vowels; and these characters express sounds, and a sound may comprise a short syllable. I learned to read by this system in four lessons. I first read in public in Mornington Crescent. For the first fortnight or three weeks I took from two shillings and sixpence to two shillings and ninepence a day – one day I took three shillings. My receipts then fell to something less than eighteen pence a day, and have been gradually falling ever since. Since the 1st of January, this year, I haven't averaged more than two and sixpence a week by my street reading and writing.

My wife earns three or four shillings a week with her needle, slaving with a 'sweater' to a shirtmaker. I have never read anywhere but in Euston Square and Mornington Crescent. On Whit Monday I made two shillings and a half-penny and that, I assure you, I reckon real good holiday earnings; and I read until I was hoarse with it. Once I counted at Mornington Crescent, as closely as I could, just out of curiosity and to wile away the time, above 2,000 persons, who passed and re-passed without giving me a halfpenny. The working people are my best friends, most decidedly. I am tired of the streets; besides, being half-starved. There are now five or six blind men about London, who read in the streets. We can read nothing but the Scriptures, as 'blind printing' – so it's sometimes called – has only been used in the Scriptures. I write also in the streets, as well as read. I use Wedgwood's manifold writer. I write verses from Scripture. There was no teaching necessary for this. I trace the letters from my knowledge of them when I could see. I believe I am the only blind man who writes in the streets.[30]

A Maker of Eyes

A curious part of the street toy business is the sale of dolls, and especially that odd branch of it, dolls'-eye making. There are only two persons following this business in London, and by the most intelligent of these I was furnished with the following curious information:

I make all kinds of eyes, both dolls' and human eyes; birds' eyes are mostly manufactured in Birmingham, and as you say, sir, bulls' eyes at the confectioner's. Of dolls' eyes there are two sorts, the common and the natural, as we call it. The common are simply small hollow glass spheres, made of white enamel, and coloured either black or blue, for only two colours of these are made. The bettermost dolls' eyes, or the natural ones, are made in a superior manner, but after a similar fashion to the commoner sort. The price of the common black and blue dolls' eyes is five shillings for twelve dozen pair. We make very few of the bettermost kind, or natural eyes for dolls, for the price of those is about fourpence a pair, but they are only for the very best dolls. Average it throughout the year, a journeyman dolls'-eye maker earns about thirty shillings a week. The common dolls' eyes were twelve shillings the twelve dozen pairs twenty-five years ago, but now they are only five shillings. The decrease of the price is owing to competition, for though there are only two of us in the trade in London, still the other party is always pushing his eyes and underselling our'n. Immediately the demand ceases at all, he goes round the trade with his eyes in a box, and offers them at a lower figure than in the regular season, and so the prices have been falling every year. There is a brisk and a slack season in our business, as well as in most others. After the Christmas holidays up to March we have generally little to do, but from that time eyes begin to look up a bit, and the business remains pretty good till the end of October.

Where we make one pair of eyes for home consumption, we make ten for exportation; a great many eyes go abroad. Yes, I suppose we should be soon over-populated with dolls if a great number of them were not to emigrate every year. The annual increase of dolls goes on at an alarming rate. As you say, sir, the yearly rate of mortality must be very high, to be sure, but still it's nothing to the rate at which they are brought into the world. They can't make wax dolls in America, sir, so we ship off a great many there. The reason why they can't produce dolls in America is owing to the climate. The wax won't set in very hot weather, and it cracks in extreme cold. I knew a party who went out to the United

States to start as doll-maker. He took several gross of my eyes with him, but he couldn't succeed. The eyes that we make for Spanish America are all black. A blue-eyed doll wouldn't sell at all there. Here, however, nothing but blue eyes goes down; that's because it's the colour of the Queen's eyes, and she sets the fashion in our eyes as in other things. We make the same kind of eyes for the gutta-percha dolls as for the wax. It is true, the gutta-percha complexion isn't particularly clear; nevertheless, the eyes I make for the washable faces are all of the natural tint, and if the guttapercha dolls look rather bilious, why I ain't a going to make my eyes look bilious to match.

I also make human eyes. These are two cases; in the one I have black and hazel, and in the other blue and grey.

Here the man took the lids off a couple of boxes, about as big as binnacles that stood on the table: they each contained 190 different eyes, and so like nature, that the effect produced upon a person unaccustomed to the sight was most peculiar, and far from pleasant. The whole of the 380 optics all seemed to be staring directly at the spectator, and occasioned a feeling somewhat similar to the bewilderment one experiences on suddenly becoming an object of general notice; as if the eyes, indeed, of a whole lecture-room were crammed into a few square inches, and all turned full upon you. The eyes of the whole world, as we say, literally appeared to be fixed upon one, and it was almost impossible at first to look at them without instinctively averting the head. The hundred eyes of Argus were positively insignificant in comparison to the 380 belonging to the human eye-maker.

'Here you see are the ladies' eyes,' he continued, taking one from the blue-eye tray.

You see there's more sparkle and brilliance about them than the gentlemen's. Here's two different ladies' eyes; they belong to fine-looking young women, both of them. When a lady or gentleman comes to us for an eye, we are obliged to have a sitting just like a portrait-painter. We take no sketch, but study the tints of the perfect eye. There are a number of eyes come over from France, but these are generally what we call misfits; they are sold cheap, and seldom match the other eye. Again, from not fitting tight over the ball like those that are made expressly for the person, they seldom move 'consentaneously', as it is termed, with the natural eye, and have therefore a very unpleasant and fixed stare, worse almost than the defective eye itself. Now, the eyes we make move so freely, and have such a natural appearance, that I can assure you a gentleman who had one of his from me passed nine doctors without the deception being detected. There is a lady customer of mine who has been married three years to her husband, and I believe he doesn't know that she has a false eye to this day.

The generality of persons whom we serve take out their eyes when they go to bed, and sleep with them either under their pillow, or else in a tumbler of water on the toilet-table at their side. Most married ladies, however, never take their eyes out at all.

Some people wear out a false eye in half the time of others. This doesn't arise from the greater use of them, or rolling them about, but from the increased secretion of the tears, which act on the false eye like acid on metal, and so corrodes and roughens the surface. This roughness produces inflammation, and then a new eye becomes necessary. The Scotch lose a great many eyes, why I cannot say; and the men in this country lose more eyes, nearly two to one. We generally make only one eye, but I did once make two false eyes for a widow lady. She lost one first, and we repaired the loss so well, that on her losing the other eye she got us to make her a second.

False eyes are a great charity to servants. If they lose an eye no one will engage them. In Paris there is a charitable institution for the supply of false eyes to the poor; and I really think, if there was a similar establishment in this country for furnishing artificial eyes to those whose bread depends on their looks, like servants, it would do a great deal of good. We always supplies eyes to such people at half-price. My usual price is two pounds two shillings for one of my best eyes. That eye is a couple of guineas, and as fine an eye as you would wish to see in any young woman's head. I suppose we make from 300 to 400 false eyes every year. The great art in making a false eye is in polishing the edges quite smooth. Of dolls' eyes we make about 6,000 dozen pairs of the common ones every year. I take it that there are near upon 24,000 dozen, or more than a quarter of a million, pairs of all sorts of dolls' eyes made annually in London.[31]

The Senses of the Blind

Many blind men can, I am told, distinguish between the several kinds of wood by touch alone. Mahogany, oak, ash, elm, deal, they say, have all a different feel. They declare it is quite ridiculous, the common report, that blind people can discern colours by the touch.

One of my informants, who assured me that he was considered to be one of the cleverest of blind people, told me that he had made several experiments on this subject, and never could distinguish the least difference between black or red, or white, or yellow, or blue, or, indeed, any of the mixed colours. 'My wife,' said one, went blind so young, that she doesn't never remember having seen the light; and I am often sorry for her that she has no idea of what a beautiful thing light or colours is. We often talk about it together, and then she goes a little bit melancholy, because I can't make her understand what the daylight is like, or the great delight that there is in seeing it. I've often asked whether she knows that the daylight and the candle-light is of different colours, and she has told me she thinks they are the same; but then she has no notion of colours at all. Now, it's such people as these I pities.

I told the blind man of Sanderson's wonderful effect of imagination in conceiving that the art of seeing was similar to that of a series of threads being drawn from the distant object to the eye; and he was delighted with the explanation, saying, 'he could hardly tell how a born blind man could come at such an idea'. On talking with this man, he told me he remembered having seen a looking-glass once – his mother was standing putting her cap on before it, and he thought he never saw anything so pretty as the reflection of the half-mourning gown she had on, and the white feathery pattern upon it (he was five years old then). He also remembered having seen his shadow, and following it across the street; these were the only two objects he can call to mind. He told me that he knew many blind men who could not comprehend how things could be seen, round or square, *all at once;* they are obliged, they say, to pass their fingers all over them; and how it is that the shape of a thing can be known in an instant, they cannot possibly imagine. I found out that this blind man fancied the looking-glass reflected only one object at once – only the object that was immediately in front of it; and when I told him that, looking in the glass, I could see everything in the room, and even himself, with my back turned towards him, he smiled with agreeable astonishment. He said, 'You see how little I have thought about the matter.' There was a blind woman of his acquaintance, he informed me, who could thread the smallest needle with the finest hair in a minute, and never miss once. 'She'll do it in a second. Many blind women thread their needles with their tongues; the woman who stitches by the Polytechnic always does so.' My informant was very fond of music. One of the blind makes his own teeth, he told me; his front ones have all been replaced by one long bit of bone which he has fastened to the stumps of his two eye teeth; he makes them out of any old bit of bone he can pick up. He files them and drills a hole through them to fasten them into his head, and eats his food with them. He is obliged to have teeth because he plays the clarionet in the street. 'Music,' he said, 'is our only enjoyment, we all like to listen to it and learn it'. It affects them greatly, they tell me, and if a lively tune is played, they can hardly help dancing. 'Many a tune I've danced to so that I could hardly walk the next day', said one.

Almost all of the blind men are clever at reckoning. It seems to come natural to them after the loss of their sight. By counting they say they spend many a dull hour – it appears to be all mental arithmetic with them, for they never aid their calculations by their fingers or any signs whatever. My informant knew a blind man who could reckon on what day it was new moon for a hundred years back, or when it will be new moon a century to come – he had never had a book read to him on the subject in his life – he was one of the blind wandering musicians. My informant told me he often sits for hours and calculates how many quarters of ounces there are in a ship-load of tea, and such like things. Many of the blind are very partial to the smell of flowers. My informant knew one blind man about the streets who always would have some kind of smelling flowers in his room.[32]

'I can't see the least light in the world – not the brightest sun that ever shone,' said another blind man. 'I have pressed my eye-balls – they are quite decayed, you see; but I have pushed them in, and they have merely hurt me, and the water has run from them faster than ever. I have never seen any colours when I did so.' (This question was asked to discover whether the illusion called 'peacock's feathers' could still be produced by pressure on the nerve.)

I have been struck on the eye since I have been blind, and then I have seen a flash of fire like lightning. I know it's been like that, because I've seen the lightning sometimes, when it's been very vivid, even since I was stone blind. It was terrible pain when I was struck on the eye. A man one day was carrying some chairs along the street, and struck me right in the eyeball with the end of the leg of one of the chairs; and I fell to the ground with the pain. I thought my heart was coming out of my mouth; then I saw the brightest flash that ever I saw, either before or since I was blind. [I irritated the ball of the eye with the object of discovering whether the nerve was decayed, but found it impossible to produce any luminous impression – though I suspect this arose principally from the difficulty of getting him to direct his eye in the proper direction.]

I know the difference of colours, because I remember them; but I can't distinguish them by my touch, nor do I think that any blind man in the world ever could. I have heard of blind people playing at cards, but it's impossible they can do so any other way than by having them marked. I know many that plays cards that way.

He was given two similar substances, but of different colours, to feel, but could not distinguish between them – both were the same to him, he said,

With the exception that one felt stiffer than the other. I know hundreds of people myself – and they know hundreds more – and none of us has ever heard of one that could tell colours by the feel. There's blind people in the school can tell the colours of their rods; but they do so by putting their tongue to them, and so they can distinguish them that's been dipped in copper from them that hasn't. I know blind people can take a clock to pieces, and put it together again, as well as any person that can see. Blind people gets angry when they hear people talk of persons seeing with their fingers. A man has told me that a blind person in St James's workhouse could read the newspaper with his fingers, but that, the blind know, is quite impossible.[33]

A Blind Needle Seller

Well, sir, I come out of the hospital stone blind, and have been in darkness ever since, and that's near upon ten years ago. I often dream of colours, and see the most delightful pictures in the world; nothing that I ever beheld with my eyes can equal them – they're so brilliant, and clear and beautiful. I see then the features and figures of all my old friends, and I can't tell you how pleasurable it is to me. When I have such dreams they so excite me that I am ill all the next day. I often see, too, the fields, with the cows grazing on a beautiful green pasture, and the flowers, just at twilight like, closing up their blossoms as they do. I never dream of rivers; nor do I ever remember seeing a field of corn in my visions; it's strange I never dreamt in any shape of the corn or the rivers, but maybe I didn't take so much notice of them as of the others. Sometimes I see the sky, and very often indeed there's a rainbow in it, with all kinds of beautiful colours. The sun is a thing I often dream about seeing, going down like a ball of fire at the close of the day. I never dreamt of the stars, nor the moon – it's mostly bright colours that I see.

I have been under all the oculists I could hear of – Mr. Turnbull, in Russell Square, but he did me no good; then I went to Charing Cross, under Mr. Guthrie, and he gave me a blind certificate, and made me a present of half-a-sovereign; he told me not to have my eyes tampered with again, as the optic nerve was totally decayed. Oh, yes; if I had all the riches in the world I'd give them every one to get my sight back, for it's the greatest pressure to me to be in darkness. God help me! I know I am a sinner, and believe I'm so afflicted on account of my sins. No, sir, it's nothing like when you shut your eyes; when I had my sight, and closed mine, I remember I could still see the light through the lids, the very same as when you hold your hand up before the candle; but mine's far darker than that – pitch black. I see a dark mass like before me, and never any change – everlasting darkness, and no chance of a light or shade in this world. But I feel consolated somehow, now it is settled; although it's a very poor comfort after all... Shortly after my becoming quite blind, I found all my other senses much quickened – my hearing – feeling – and reckoning. I got to like music very much indeed; it seemed to elevate me – to animate and cheer me much more than it did before, and so much so now, that when it ceases, I feel duller than ever. It sounds as if it was in a wilderness to me – I can't tell why, but that's all I can compare it to; as if I was quite alone with it. My smell and taste is very acute. [He was given some violets to smell.] Oh, that's beautiful, very reviving indeed. Often of an evening, I can see things in my imagination, and that's why I like to sit alone then; for of all the beautiful thoughts that ever a man possessed, there's none to equal a blind man's, when he's by hisself.

I don't see my early home, but occurrences that has recently took place. I see them all plain before me, in colours as vivid as if I had my sight again, and the people all dressed in the fashion of my time; the clothes seem to make a great impression on me, and I often sit and see in my mind master tailors trying a coat on a gentleman, and pulling it here and there. The figures keep passing before me like soldiers, and often I'm so took by them that I forget I'm blind, and turn my head round to look after them as they pass by me. But that sort of thinking would throw me into a melancholy – it's too exciting while it lasts, and then leaves me dreadful dull afterwards. I have got much more melancholy since my blindness; before then, I was not seriously given, but now I find great consolation in religion. I think my blindness is sent to try my patience and resignation, and I pray to the Almighty to give me strength to bear with my affliction. I was quick and hot-tempered before I was blind, but since then, I have got less hasty like; all other troubles appears nothing to me. Sometimes I revile against my affliction – too frequently – but that is at my thoughtless moments, for when I'm calm and serious, I feel thankful that the Almighty has touched me with his correcting rod, and then I'm happy and at peace with all the world. If I had run my race, and not been stopped, I might never have believed there was a God.[34]

Some Blind Musicians

A stout, hale-looking blind man, dressed very decently in coloured clothes, and scrupulously clean, gave me the following details:

I am one of the three blind Scotchmen who go about the streets in company, playing the violoncello, clarionet, and flute. We are really Highlanders, and can all speak Gaelic; but a good many London Highlanders are Irish. I have been thirty years in the streets of London; one of my mates has been forty years – he's sixty-nine; the other has been thirty years. I became partially blind, through an inflammation, when I was fourteen, and was stone-blind when I was twenty-two. Before I was totally blind I came to London, travelling up with the help of my bagpipes, guided by a little boy. I settled in London, finding it a big place, where a man could do well at that time, and I took a turn every now and then into the country. I could make fourteen shillings a week, winter and summer through, thirty years ago, by playing in the streets; now I can't make six shillings a week, take winter and summer. I met my two mates, who are both blind men, – both came to England for the same reason as I did, – in my journeyings in London; and at last we agreed to go together – that's twenty years ago. We've been together, on and off, ever since. Sometimes, one of us will take a turn round the coast of Kent, and another round the coast of Devon; and then join again in London, or meet by accident. We have always agreed very well, and never fought. We – I mean the street-blind – tried to maintain a burying and sick-club of our own; but we were always too poor. We live in rooms. I don't know one blind musician who lives in a lodging-house. I myself know a dozen blind men, now performing in the streets of London; these are not all exactly blind, but about as bad; the most are stone-blind. The blind musicians are chiefly married men. I don't know one who lives with a woman unmarried. The loss of sight changes a man. He doesn't think of women, and women don't think of him.

We are of a religious turn, too, generally. I am a Roman Catholic; but the other Scotch blind men here are Presbyterians. The Scotch in London are our good friends, because they give us a little sum altogether, perhaps; but the English working-people are our main support: it is by them we live, and I always found them kind and liberal – the most liberal in the world as I know. Through Marylebone is our best round, and Saturday night our best time. We play all three together. 'Johnny Cope' is our best-liked tune. I think the blind Scotchmen don't come to play in London now. I can remember many blind Scotch musicians, or pipers, in London: they are all dead now! The trade's dead too – it is so! When we thought of forming the blind club, there was never more than a dozen members. These were two basket-makers, one mat-maker, four violin-players, myself, and my two mates; which was the number when it dropped for want of funds; that's now fifteen years ago. We were to pay a shilling a month; and sick members were to have five shillings a week, when they'd paid two years. Our other rules were the same as other clubs, I believe.

The blind musicians now in London are we three: Cohen, a Jew, who plays the violin; Randolph, an Englishman, who plays the violin elegantly; Williams, a harp player; Treadwell, violin again; Harris, violin (but he plays more in public-houses); Richardson, the flute; McBrayne, bagpipes; Charles, bagpipes; Kerry, violin: that's all I know myself. There's a good many blind who play at the sailors' dances, Wapping and Deptford way. We seldom hire children to lead us in the streets; we have plenty of our own, generally – I have five! Our wives are generally women who have their eyesight; but some blind men – I know one couple – marry blind women.[35]

One of the most deserving and peculiar of the street musicians was an old lady who played upon a hurdy-gurdy. She had been about the streets of London for upwards of forty years, and being blind, had had during that period four guides, and worn out three instruments. Her cheerfulness, considering her privation and precarious mode of life, was extraordinary. Her love of truth, and the extreme simplicity of her nature, were almost childlike. Like the generality of blind people, she had a deep sense of religion, and her charity for a woman in her station of life was something marvellous; for, though living on alms, she herself had, I was told, two or three little pensioners. When questioned on this subject, she laughed the matter off as a jest, though I was assured of the truth of the fact. Her attention to her guide was most marked. If a cup of tea was given to her after her day's rounds, she would be sure to turn to the poor creature who led her about, and ask, 'You comfortable, Liza?' or, 'Is your tea to your liking, Liza?'

When conveyed to Mr. Beard's establishment to have her daguerreotype taken, she for the first time in her life rode in a cab; and then her fear at being pulled 'back'ards' as she termed it (for she sat with her back to the horse), was almost painful. She felt about for something to lay hold of, and did not appear comfortable until she had a firm grasp of the pocket. After her alarm had in a measure subsided, she turned to her guide and said, 'We must put up with those trials, Liza.' In a short time, however, she began to find the ride pleasant enough. 'Very nice, ain't it Liza?' she said, 'But I shouldn't like to ride on them steamboats, they say they're shocking dangerous; and as for them railways, I've heard tell they're dreadful; but these cabs, Liza, is very nice.' On the road she was continually asking 'Liza' where they were, and wondering at the rapidity at which they travelled. 'Ah!' she said, laughing, 'if I had one of these here cabs, my 'rounds' would soon be over.' Whilst ascending the high flight of stairs that led to the portrait rooms, she laughed at every proposal made to her to rest. 'There's twice as many stairs as these to our church, ain't there, Liza?' she replied when pressed. When the portrait was finished she expressed a wish to feel it.

The following is the history of her life, as she herself related it, answering to the variety of questions put to her on the subject:

I was born the 4th April, 1786 (it was Good Friday that year), at a small chandler's shop, facing the White Horse, Stuart's Rents, Drury Lane. Father was a hatter, and mother an artificial-flower maker and feather finisher. When I was but a day old, the nurse took me out of the warm bed and carried me to the window, to show some people how like I was to father. The cold flew to my eyes and I caught inflammation in them. Owing to mother being forced to be from home all day at her work, I was put out to dry-nurse when I was three weeks old. My eyes were then very bad, by all accounts, and some neighbours told the woman I was with, that Turner's cerate would do them good. She got some and put it on my eyes, and when poor mother came to suckle me at her dinner-hour, my eyes was all 'a gore of blood'. From that time I never see afterwards. She did it, poor woman, for the best; it was no fault of her'n, and I'm sure I bears her no malice for it. I stayed at home with mother until I was thirteen, when I was put to the Blind School, but I only kept there nine months; they turned me out because I was not clever with my hands, and I could not learn to spin or make sash-lines; my hands was ocker'd like. I had not been used at home to do anything for myself, not even to dress myself. Mother was always out at her work, so she could not learn me, and no one else would, so that's how it was I was turned out. I then went back to my mother, and kept with her till her death. I well remember that; I heard her last. When she died I was just sixteen year old.

I was sent to the Union – Pancridge Union it was – and father with me (for he was ill at the time). He died too, and left me, in seven weeks after mother. When they was both gone, I felt I had lost my only friends, and that I was all alone in the world and blind. But, take it altogether, the world has been very good to me, and I have much to thank God for and the good woman I am with. I missed mother the most, she was so kind to me; there was no-one like her; no, not even father. I was kept in the Union until I was twenty; the parish paid for my learning the cymbal. God bless them for it, I say. A poor woman in the workhouse first asked me to learn music; she said it would always be a bit of bread for me; I did as she told me, and I thank her to this day for it. It took me just five months to learn the cymbal, if you please the hurdygurdy ain't its right name.

The first tune I ever played was 'God save the King', the Queen as is now; then 'Harlequin Hamlet', that took me a long time to get off; it was three weeks before they put me on a new one. I then learnt 'Moll Brook'; then I did the 'Turnpike-gate' and 'Patrick's day in the morning'; all of them I learnt in the Union. I got a poor man to teach me the 'New-rigged ship', I soon learnt it, because it was an easy tune. Two-and-forty years ago I played 'The Gal I left behind me'. A woman learnt it me; she played my cymbal and I listened, and so got it. 'Oh, Susannah!' I learnt myself by hearing it on the organ. I always try and listen to a new tune when I am in the street, and get it off if I can: it's my bread. I waited to hear one today, quite a new one, but I didn't like it, so I went on. 'Hasten to the Wedding' is my favourite; I played it years ago, and play it still. I like 'Where have you been all the night?'; it's a Scotch tune. The woman as persuaded me to learn the cymbal took me out of the Union with her; I lived with her, and she led me about the streets. When she died I took her daughter for my guide. She walked with me for more than five-and-twenty year, and she might have been with me to this day, but she took to drinking and killed herself with it. She behaved very bad to me at last, for as soon as we got a few halfpence she used to go into the public and spend it all; and many a time I'm sure she's been too tipsy to take me home. One night I remember she rolled into the road at Kensington, and as near pulled me with her. We was both locked up in the station-house, for she couldn't stand for liquor, and I was obligated to wait till she could lead me home. It was very cruel of her to treat me so, but, poor creature, she's gone, and I forgive her I'm sure. I'd many guides arter her, but none of them was honest like Liza is: I don't think she'd rob me of a farden. Would you, Liza?

Yes, I've my reg'lar rounds, and I've kept to 'em for near upon fifty year. All the children like to hear me coming along, for I always plays my cymbal as I goes. At Kentish Town they calls me Mrs. Tuesday, and at Kensington I'm Mrs. Friday, and so on. At some places they likes polkas, but at one house I plays at in Kensington they always ask me for 'Haste to the Wedding'. No, the cymbal isn't very hard to play; the only thing is, you must be very particular that the works is covered up, or the halfpence is apt to drop in. King David, they say, played on one of those here instruments. We're very tired by night-time; ain't we, Liza? But when I gets home the good woman I lodges with has always a bit of something for me to eat with my cup of tea. She's a good soul, and keeps me tidy and clean. I helps her all I can; when I come in, I carries her a pail of water upstairs, and suchlike. Many ladies as has known me since they was children allows me a trifle. One maiden lady near Brunswick Square has given me sixpence a week for many a year, and another allows me eighteenpence a fortnight; so that, one way and another, I am very comfortable, and I've much to be thankful for.

It was during one of old Sarah's journeys that an accident occurred, which ultimately deprived London of the well-known old hurdygurdy woman. In crossing Seymour Street, she and her guide Liza were knocked down by a cab, as it suddenly turned a corner. They were picked up and placed in the vehicle (the poor guide dead, and Sarah with her limbs broken), and carried to the University Hospital. Old Sarah's description of that ride is more terrible and tragic than I can hope to make out to you. The poor blind creature was ignorant of the fate of her guide, she afterwards told us, and kept begging and praying to Liza to speak to her as the vehicle conveyed them to the asylum. She shook her, she said, and entreated her to say if she was hurt, but not a word was spoken in answer, and then she felt how terrible a privation was her blindness; and it was not until they reached the hospital, and they were lifted from the cab, that she knew, as she heard the people whisper to one another, that her faithful attendant was dead. In telling us this, the good old soul forgot her own sufferings for the time, as she lay with both her legs broken beneath the hooped bed-clothes of the hospital bed; and when, after many long weeks, she left the medical asylum, she was unable to continue her playing on the hurdy-gurdy, her hand being now needed for the crutch that was requisite to bear her on her rounds.

The shock, however, had been too much for the poor old creature's feeble nature to rally against, and though she continued to hobble round to the houses of the kind people who had for years allowed her a few pence per week, and went limping along musicless through the streets for some months after she left the hospital, yet her little remaining strength at length failed her, and she took to her bed in a room in Bell Court, Gray's Inn Lane, never to rise from it again.[36]

Notes

All references are to *London Labour and the London Poor*, by Henry Mayhew, Griffin, Bohn and Company, 1861–2, vols 1–3

1. Vol 1, p. 435
2. Vol 3, p. 30
3. Vol 3, p. 9
4. Vol 2, p. 431
5. Vol 2, p. 248
6. Vol 1, p. 71
7. Vol 1, p. 57
8. Vol 3, p. 415
9. Vol 3, p. 425
10. Vol 2, p. 506
11. Vol 3, p. 413
12. Vol 1, p. 358
13. Vol 2, p. 430
14. Vol 1, p. 483
15. Vol 1, p. 091
16. Vol 1, p. 330
17. Vol 2, p. 487
18. Vol 3, p. 88
19. Vol 2, p. 489
20. Vol 3, p. 213
21. Vol 2, p. 304
22. Vol 2, p. 493
23. Vol 2, p. 368
24. Vol 2, p. 471
25. Vol 1, p. 162
26. Vol 3, p. 242
27. Vol 3, p. 253
28. Vol 1, p. 100
29. Vol 3, p. 213
30. Vol 3, p. 154
31. Vol 3, p. 231
32. Vol 1, p. 401
33. Vol 1, p. 401
34. Vol 1, p. 342
35. Vol 3, p. 162
36. Vol 3, p. 159

Biographical note

Henry Mayhew was an English journalist, author and social reformer. Born in London in 1812, he was educated at Westminster School and served as a midshipman in the East India Company. On his return to England he briefly underwent legal training before taking up freelance writing, fleeing to Paris in 1835 to dodge his creditors.

In 1841 Mayhew cofounded the satirical news magazine *Punch*, although he was directly associated with it for only a short period. From 1842 he also made contributions to the *Illustrated London News*, becoming financially secure enough to settle his debts, return to England and marry.

In 1849, after a serious cholera outbreak killed over 10,000 Londoners, Mayhew began observing and conducting interviews with the poor working people of London, initially for a series of articles in the *Morning Chronicle*. These articles went into meticulous detail concerning the lives, living arrangements and occupations of the working classes, as well as the daily struggle of itinerants and beggars. Mayhew's articles were collected in book form in 1851, in the three volumes of *London Labour and the London Poor*. The 1861 edition added a fourth volume that focused on petty criminals, prostitutes and vagrants. Mayhew's work exerted considerable influence over radicals and socialists, but also over Charles Dickens, whose novels featured characters inspired by some of Mayhew's subjects.

Henry Mayhew died in 1887 and was buried in Kensal Green.

HESPERUS PRESS

Hesperus Press is committed to bringing near what is far – far both in space and time. Works written by the greatest authors, and unjustly neglected or simply little known in the English-speaking world, are made accessible through new translations and a completely fresh editorial approach. Through these classic works, the reader is introduced to the greatest writers from all times and all cultures.

For more information on Hesperus Press, please visit our website: **www.hesperuspress.com**